BUILDING SEARCH

SEARCH

Tactics For The Patrol Officer

BUILDING SEARCH
Tactics For The Patrol Officer

By
James D. Stalnaker

Foreword by
Lt. Al Baker, NYPD (Ret.)

VARRO
P R E S S

BUILDING SEARCH
Tactics For The Patrol Officer

James D. Stalnaker

VARRO PRESS
P.O. Box 8413
Shawnee Mission, Kansas 66208 USA
Tel: 913-385-2034 ~ Fax: 913-385-2039 ~ Web: www.varropress.com

Publisher's Cataloging-in-Publication

Stalnaker; James D.

Building search : tactics for the patrol officer / James D. Stalnaker. - 1st ed. -- Shawnee Mission, Kan. : Varro Press, 2005.

p. ; cm.

ISBN: 1-888644-40-0

1. Crime scene searches. 2. Criminal investigation. 3. Searches and seizures. 4. Criminal procedure. I. Title.

HV8073 . S73 2005   2004117918
363.25--dc22   0506

Printed and bound in the United States

TABLE OF CONTENTS

WARNING & DISCLAIMER.
READ THIS BEFORE YOU CONTINUE.

The author and publisher have made every effort to ensure the accuracy of the information contained in this book. The author and publisher of this book disclaim any liability, including liability for negligence, for any personal injury, property damage, or any other loss, damage, cost, claim, or expense including claims for consequential damages that the reader or others may suffer from following any of the suggestions, advice, or methods of instruction provided in this book. The reader of this book recognizes and accepts this disclaimer of liability by the author and the publisher, and the reader ASSUMES THE RISK of using firearms and/or attempting to defend himself/herself or others from criminal attack. The DISCLAIMER OF LIABILITY by the author and the publisher and ASSUMPTION OF RISK by the reader is made and communicated in part because of what is described below:

You need to learn the laws of your own jurisdiction(s).

You need to learn the policies of your agency.

Reading and following the advice in this book is no guarantee that you won't be successfully prosecuted or sued.

Attempting to defend yourself and others is dangerous.

Following the tactics in this book will not guarantee you or others won't be hurt.

Handling firearms is dangerous and you can't learn it all properly from this - or any other - book. Get hands on instruction from a qualified instructor before you start.

Searching a building is inherently dangerous. This book offers tactical suggestions but the reader should not attempt an actual search until you have been properly trained by a qualiified instructor.

You should never attempt to search a building alone.

Because every agency is different, the ideas expressed in this book are presented as general information and guidelines only, and are not intended to be interpreted as policy, procedures, or absolutes.

DEDICATION

This book is dedicated to all the silent heroes,
the thousands of men and women who place their lives on
the line every day in the performance of their duties as law
enforcement officers to protect their communities against
those who would prey on the innocent and unprotected.

I began writing this book with the above dedication. At that
time I could not imagine that on September 11, 2001 many of
our brothers and sisters would be called on to make the ulti-
mate sacrifice. They died while trying to rescue thousands of
their fellow citizens who were trapped in burning buildings,
lost to the terror caused by a barbaric attack on our country.

We should never forget the heroism those brave and
dedicated officers displayed that day in New York City and
Washington, D.C. Without hesitation many of those silent
heroes stepped forward and did what they knew they had to do.
They went forth to help others in desperate need knowing that
their actions could cost them their own lives. To those coura-
geous souls who sacrificed all they had to save others, I offer
this special dedication.

Thanks to all of the fallen silent heroes of September 11, 2001
for your unselfish sacrifice and unwavering dedication to
the protection of the innocent and unprotected, our country,
and the law enforcement profession. May God keep you
in his graces and watch over those you left behind.

James D. Stalnaker

ACKNOWLEDGMENTS

The writing of this book has been a long process. Without the patience, understanding and encouragement of my lovely wife Laurie, it would never have been written. Thank you hon for your never-ending support.

I would also like to thank some of the many people who helped, encouraged, and cajoled me to get it done.

Lt Al Baker, NYPD (Ret.) who wrote the Foreword to this book. What an honor! True warriors such as Al are few and far between. If you read Al's Foreword you will recognize his concern for your safety, and the caring, understanding, and dedication he has brought to our profession as an active operator with the NYPD ESU, and as a mentor and teacher when he was with Armor Holdings and later the Bureau of Alcohol, Tobacco and Firearms as one of their lead instructors. He continues this commitment and dedication through his current work developing the revolutionary body armor device, the Baker BatShield. If you ever have the opportunity to take one of Al's classes on the use of ballistic shields, do it, otherwise you will miss some excellent training and insights into tactics and officer safety. This is must attend training for SWAT and patrol officers. Thanks Al, you truly overwhelmed me with your words.

Sergeant Robert Higgins (Ret.), San Bernardino County California Sheriff's Department. Bob was the first to proofread my work and encouraged me to continue. Thanks Bob, you're a true friend.

Detective Harry Hatch, San Bernardino County California Sheriff's Department. Not only is Harry a good friend and fellow instructor, but he went out of his way and graciously shared with me his expertise in building clearing methods.

David Starling of Santa Monica, CA. David's support of the law enforcement profession is reflected in the photographs he so painstakingly took to get my message in pictures. Great job David!

Edward P. Dugan III, one of my best friends. Without his harassment and encouragement I probably wouldn't have completed this project. Thanks again Ed. I don't really know what it is you do, but whatever it is, be safe. Oh yeah, and continue to get rich from it.

Sergeant Joseph Paskvan, (Ret.), Cleveland, Ohio Police Department. Another one of my best friends, he continuously harassed and encouraged me to complete this project before I died. Joe backed up his harassment and encouragement by helping edit this book and offered valuable advice from another agency's point of view. Thanks Joe, I ain't dead yet.

Blair Gluba, (Ret.), Naval Investigative Service, for his friendship, encouragement, and sharing his thoughts and ideas with me in writing this book.

Richard Machowicz, U.S. Navy SEAL (Ret.) whom I met while writing this book. He shared with me his insight into achieving goals in life, in particular, winning at all that we do, which is the premise of this book, to always win and go home at the end of our shifts. Oh, by the way, he's the "bad-ass" in the pictures. Richard's book, *Unleashing the Warrior Within* is well worth reading. It will help you get and maintain your winning mindset.

Michael Nossaman, my publisher, the founder of TREXPO and President of VARRO PRESS. Thanks for letting me be part of your organization, for your encouragement and endless suggestions, and all the time you spent editing my manuscript to, "make it better."

Marcia Nossaman, Mike's gracious wife and partner who patiently and carefully proofread this book so many times. Thank you for your many helpful suggestions and for catching all those pesky typos.

The officers and friends mentioned above are the true epitome of professionalism and dedication to helping others win and survive in our profession. Thanks guys!

And finally, thanks to the literally hundreds of officers, cadets, peers, team members, and students with whom I have had the privilege to work over the years, for giving me your time and attention during my classes, and by applying the principles, tactics, and techniques I have offered in this book both in training and real life situations. I am indebted to all of you for your honest and forthright evaluations and suggestions about my building search principles. Thank you for helping me to get it right for those who will read this book and learn from it. Your contribution will help other officers to conduct better and safer building searches.

James D. Stalnaker

FOREWORD

By Al Baker

The crushed gray gravel crunched loudly under my feet as I navigated the winding paths of Vanderveer park late that sizzling Friday. Hastily, I reached the steps of our family's modest house with a shiny tin badge newly tucked in my pocket. Sworn in for mere hours, I would sprint past the memorable aroma of Mom's simmering pot roast and bolt upstairs to my room, where I would rip the palm-sized shield out of my jeans and stare, with prideful disbelief, at its awesome inscription: *Police Officer—City of New York.* They'd given me a brand new pistol too that day. Still in the box. My gaze floated out the window to the rectangular city-block park across the Brooklyn street above the thick, green contours of the Oaks and Maples, and I reflected. It was pretty basic.

There'd be no modern police radios. As foot patrolmen, we'd have no partners. There were no such things as bullet-proof vests. We never heard of speedloaders. Telephones had no *"911"*. They issued us wooden sticks and nickel-plated whistles and they sent us out on the streets—alone. There was no pepper spray or even mace. It was pretty basic.

The academy would follow for six months: the gym, the Penal Law, the Rules and Procedures, the pistol range; the usual launch for a career in urban policing. There would be no bible of *how-to* tips on survival. It was '65 and I was 21. It was pretty basic.

When gym-master "Mr. Kleen" got us out on his varnished, hardwood floor, he'd *duck-walk* the whole recruit class around its endless perimeter—just because. I'd always wondered how it related to *walking* the beat. Once assigned to a precinct, the old hair bags of the big city force didn't say much—if they noticed you at all—except to say, "do the right thing kid." And sometimes you learned the hard way what *wasn't* the right thing. It came to be called experience. It was pretty basic.

That career would span a quarter century. Halfway through, dressed in tactical gear and readying to take the apartment of a cop-killer, my mentor, Lieutenant Larry Savage instructed: "try the lock—maybe it's open." It was. And we entered and made the collar without a struggle. Savage was a pro. It was pretty basic.

And today, in 21st century law enforcement, everything's different. Yet nothing is changed. We have the most sophisticated equipment we've ever had. We have semi-automatic weapons. We have mobile computers; high-tech communications and we have community policing. We have the best educated and perhaps the most physically fit people we ever did. We have *SWAT,* we have *DARE,* we have *America's Most Wanted* and we have *DNA.* We have the best understanding of the most complicated society we ever had. We have body armor. We have body bunkers. Yet it's still pretty basic. Or maybe it's really not basic enough after all?

And that is precisely where Captain Jim Stalnaker

appears. His new book, *BUILDING SEARCH: Tactics For The Patrol Officer* is pretty basic. Jim's book is that voice in your ear, that senior beat officer, that invisible veteran partner, that elder tribesman who cautions, advises, directs and enumerates the pitfalls of life on patrol. The work is a succinct reminder of how successful tactics for the patrol officer can be elusive yet simple; easy yet deadly when failed. Effectiveness can be measured in survival; simply signing out at the end of the shift on the return roll call. When the basics of search methods are not practiced there's a corresponding question infesting the depths of the patrol officer's inner sense which says 'Next time I'll know better'. Like the cop who lamented after discovering the straight razor taped inside the boot of his prisoner on the secondary body search at Central Booking. And the desk officer who gave that foreboding stare at the officer for what might've been. Like the pilot's refrain; *there are old pilots—there are bold pilots—but there are no old, bold pilots.* Captain Stalnaker personifies the sounds of experience which, after digesting his work, we take on patrol as we would the counsel of our most revered police veterans. It covers the basics.

The Captain hits you right in the running lights in telling the recruit: "you're it!" while painfully reminding us that 60 percent of hiding suspects are not found. As I read that line my thoughts raced back like yesterday to that Bronx attic we'd searched three times on behalf of the Narco boss's arrest warrant—with "negative results." But the dope sarge wouldn't relent: "He's in there!" he'd scream with blood vessels bulging. Then on the fourth search we'd found him—buried under a foot of loose, dusty, popcorn-like roofing insulation. They really don't want to get caught. It's why Captain Stalnaker gives us five basic search rules up front. He knows cops can't bring the whole manual of procedure with them on the street—he knows what "KISS" means. He's lived the consequences.

On equipment, the basics are enumerated with advice that's just plain practical. Flashlights, radios, weapons, accessories, knives, cuffs and batons: all steeped in checklist fashion for patrol officers to evaluate—to deploy—not merely to tote. The Captain even instructs the reader on equipment not carried. It's called learning how to improvise by using items typically found on scenes. It's not merely common sense because sometimes good sense evades us under stress—it's basic clear thinking through proper planning and preparation.

He reaches the reader again with a five point basic plan for taking the call then dispatches you to the scene perimeter with a straightforward, four-point rationale for containment and "invisible deployment." Pre-planning then guides the searcher's tactics while entry and movement through buildings covers sound uncomplicated search methods. The Captain winds up his basic tactics with a menu of entries blended with good team options based on simplicity and safety forming common denominators. In developing search tactics the text expertly takes the reader through a series of invaluable options: the master grip system of pointing one's weapon is excellent; communications are enumerated from radio through verbal, to non-verbal up to the concepts of triangulation. Flashlights cover Jim's "burst of light" technique, while tips on using mirrors wind up a wealth of practical search opportunities. It covers the basics.

Captain Stalnaker's six basic steps for surrender options, reminds me of the advice I religiously practiced when managing surrender tactics at scenes of exhaustive hostage-barricade operations. Again the air travel analogy applies: it's the take-offs and landings which are most troublesome. First responses and concluding tactics are when opportunities for disaster loom largest. And like the loosey-goosey surrender tactic at the conclusion of the endless siege: just when everything seems over; just when we start to relax; is just when the suspect senses weakness, indecision, and loss of control. And with no scripted tactic to depart from, confusion, danger, and surprise walk right in. It's why the Captain puts clear, precise commands as his final surrender step—he attended the debriefings on the "Good Guy's" hostage situation in Sacramento, California a few years back. The surrender was set. The negotiators all but put down their headsets. They readied for the end. But instead the whole tactic went south and the hostage takers started executing innocent captives. And it took a determined group of tactical officers to courageously bring back control. The veteran writer of this text knows too well those situations, which truly are not over until they are indeed over. Captain Stalnaker ends his must-read handbook with the fundamentals of numbering systems for building searches and perimeters. And with some constructive tips on tactical diagramming, he references the respected author, Sid Heal, thus leaving the reader with a quality blueprint for follow-up study and a healthy thirst for the avoidance of ambivalence, the rejection of complacency, and the pledge to not let boredom write your epitaph. It's pretty basic.

BUILDING SEARCH: Tactics For The Patrol Officer is the definitive primer for the newly sworn centurion as well as a constant refresher for the seasoned patrol officer. Read it through and through. Then read it again as a mental foundation for maintaining clear tactical thinking. Then take Captain Jim Stalnaker on patrol with you. Think of him as that silent partner, that voice of experience, that extra measure of safety and confidence, that will help get you returned home safely at the end of your shift, and back to that return call at the start of your next tour of duty.

Lt. Al Baker, NYPD (Ret.)

PREFACE

"Wisdom consists in being able to distinguish among dangers and make a choice of the least harmful"
—Niccolo Machiavelli

Building searches! One of the most dangerous assignments the patrol officer will undertake. When faced with the search of a building, there are myriad options for you to consider. Surprisingly, as Machiavelli suggested so many centuries ago, "distinguish among the dangers and choose the least harmful." He accurately characterized the basic premises of a tactical plan today's officer must consider to conduct a safe building search.

The theories, tactics, and techniques offered in this book are not a panacea to all building search situations. They are offered as a guide for the patrol officer on how to conduct successful building searches. More importantly, they serve as reminders to you to practice officer safety tactics by avoiding falling into bad habits.

Although this book is written primarily for the patrol officer, these tactics and concepts can be used by SWAT-teams, narcotics officers, parole or probation officers, security officers, and other specialized units where building searches or entries are a part of their mission.

INTRODUCTION

Building searches are among the most hazardous of the duties you will perform as a patrol officer, a narcotics detective, SWAT-team member or any other specialized unit you may be assigned to where one of your primary duties is to enter, secure and conduct a building search. Building searches present a maze of problems that place you in danger and at risk on a daily basis.

Generally speaking, building searches result from some type of a crime-in-progress call, usually a burglary or robbery, giving you some type of advance notice, allowing you to plan the tactics and techniques you will use when confronted with the task of searching the building. The only sure thing about a building search is that it will eventually be done and you will probably do it.

It is not enough that these calls, in and of themselves, are inherently dangerous to respond to and handle, we must add to this danger the fact that suspects in these crimes don't always "get away" before you arrive on the scene, thereby doubling the danger to you once you have arrived.

Too often we enter buildings unprepared to conduct proper searches. Therefore, you should think of the building search as a true officer safety hazard, and *the only reason you are there is to see if someone is inside, and if so, to control, contain, and arrest them.*

As patrol officers, we must remember that the "bad guys" always have the advantage. The suspects know who they are, how many, where they are hiding, and if they're armed. To make matters more difficult, even though we, as responding officers have taken every precaution in setting up the perimeter and making entry, the suspects generally know where and when we will enter the building to search for them.

There are five basic rules you should remember about suspects:

1. **The "one-plus-one" theory.** If there is one suspect, then there are probably two, if there are two, then there could be three, etc. Whether searching a building, making a traffic stop, or a pedestrian contact, this simple officer safety theory should always be followed.

2. **Two officers.** Even with the benefit of a canine team, two officers should always do building and area searches.

3. **Look into any place a small adult or child can hide.** Adults are able to contort their bodies into extremely small places when trying to avoid detection.

4. **Look up.** For some reason we don't look up when conducting searches. Quite often suspects are found hiding in high places.

5. **Stop, look and listen.** Take the time to stop, look and listen to what is going on inside the building before making entry, and while searching. Suspects may move around trying to hide better—or escape—as you are moving through the building towards them.

It is unrealistic for you to believe you will never search a building. The options available to you when confronted with a building search are not many! Generally there is only you and your fellow officers, or the canine team and you! Some agencies have policies which only permit the search of a building by a canine team. If you are a member of one of these agencies you may also be presented with a public relations problem. What happens when an irate citizen complains about your refusal to search their building for an intruder because there is no canine team available to do so?

What will you do? You can't just stand around and do nothing. Will the owner of the building understand, or care, that there is no canine team available to search their building? Of course not, and you can bet your next day off that SWAT isn't going to come out in the middle of the night to search the building for you. Realistically speaking, you will formulate some type of plan that will culminate in a building search. Unfortunately, as is typical with trying to get the job done in as little time as possible, the plan will be formulated with little, if any, tactical considerations or understanding among the officers on scene as to how the search will be conducted. To help you better understand and apply tactics, I encourage you to follow the KISS rule: Keep it Simple Stupid! I don't believe we have stupid people in our profession, but I strongly believe in the KISS theory, with a slight modification that I believe is more appropriate for our use. I would encourage you to follow my KISS rule: Keep it Safe and Simple. I believe this rule should apply to all patrol and tactical operations. If you think about it, the simpler, or easier a task is, the more successful it seems to be.

Therefore, because we often lose sight of just how dangerous a building search can be to us, and the fact we may not fully understand the true mechanics of a building search, it is for these reasons these tactics and concepts are presented. Foremost, they are predicated on the fact that **most patrol officers do have to search buildings,** and they don't always have a canine team, other special units, or tactical equipment, such as hand held ballistic shields, present or available to assist with the search. In other words "you're it," so when you do it, be sure and do it right.

We all know the Seven P's: Prior Proper Planning Prevents Piss Poor Performance. This philosophy should apply to all aspects of our law enforcement careers, particularly when it comes to officer safety tactics. When preparing to search a building, you should consider the Seven P's when answering the questions of how, when, why, and by whom the search will be conducted.

Although these four questions are relatively self-explanatory, let's take a look at them anyway. The "how" refers to the means you will use to search the building: canine only, officers only, or combination of canine and officers. The "when" refers to exactly that; when are you going to initiate the search. This also raises the question as to whether or not you are going to use any alternative tactics prior to searching, and if so, will these tactics cause undue delays to the search, or allow for possible evasion by the suspect because of delays. The "why" asks the question, why are you searching the building? Is there a known suspect inside, is there an unknown factor about the suspect, are you entering strictly to secure the building, or to search for evidence? Any of these factors dictate the degree of risk involved in your search, which must be addressed accordingly. And, the "who" refers to who will actually be searching the building, how many officers are available, who will enter the building, who will remain outside, etc.

Building Search Statistics: Statistics on building search results have remained constant over the past several years. They have shown that **60 percent of those persons hiding in a building are not found by officers** who searched without the aid of a canine team. Of those searches conducted with a canine team, the success rate has been between 96 percent and 99 percent; the type of search conducted and the environment under which the canine was used dictates the variance. Quite obviously these statistics show the canine team search is the most effective when conducted in a proper manner, and by following sound officer safety habits and search tactics. Just as obvious is the need for us to improve on our individual search skills to lower the percentage of those crooks that get away because we used poor search tactics and techniques, when we were not afforded the benefit of a canine to assist in the search.

If a canine team is available, these tactics and concepts can still be used, however, there must be a dialogue between the officers and the canine handler as to how they want the officers to assist. Normally, when a canine team is used, the second officer (you) acts as the cover officer to the handler. This allows the handler to "work" his canine and concentrate on what the canine is doing while the search is being conducted.

Alternatives and Concepts: There are, of course, alternatives to the immediate search of the building, such as announce and demand surrender and, once again, use of the canine team. As good as these two alternatives may be, and even if the suspects give up, or the canine finds a suspect or two, they do not replace the need for us to eventually enter and physically search the building.

It is with these thoughts and concerns in mind, that this book will address the concepts involved in conducting building searches where you must rely on your own capabilities, officer safety skills, training, and tactics in concert with your partner's, to produce good team work in accomplishing the mission. Because this book is designed for the patrol officer, it is important to note here that when reference is made to **"the search team"** it means **a minimum of two patrol officers** acting together to constitute a search team.

The Complexities of a Building Search: This simple floor plan shows you just how complex a building search can be.

CHAPTER 1
PREPARATION

"Be careful even in small matters"
—Miyamoto Musashi

Preparation for a safe building search starts long before you enter the building. It begins at the station while you are preparing for your shift. It starts with the proper mental attitude.

Mental Attitude: A lot has been written regarding the "mind set for survival" the "survival attitude" or the "will to survive." These "attitudes" and their philosophies and concepts are all very important and quite similar in context. However, I don't particularly like the term "survival." I prefer to use "a winning mindset." You will see why in Chapter 3, Officer Safety Reminder. I believe we begin to develop our mental attitude and survival conditioning from the moment we decide to become a cop, beginning in the academy and continuing on until we retire. Even though this is my belief, I also believe that we don't consciously think about winning on a daily basis, which leads to why I stated that your preparation begins long before you enter the building.

Quite simply, the mind must be free of outside interferences, to prepare for what the next eight hours or so will present. You need to be in a state of readiness; alert and aware of your environment and prepared to deal with whatever you may encounter during your tour of duty. You must be aware of your environment at all times. Pay attention to what is going on around you, even if you are eating or on a break. You can't afford to relax while you are on duty to the point that you are no longer aware of your surroundings and what is going on.

Preparing for Patrol: To prepare for the streets, you should review briefing logs, recent events in your beat, check the "hot sheet," talk with investigators, talk with fellow patrol officers, keep current with laws and trends from patrol briefing information, and prepare and formulate some type of mental picture as to what you intend to do for the next eight hours or so.

To help establish the right frame of mind you should commit yourself to a routine of tasks that will help ensure your safety. I know, we don't like the term "routine," but in this case it's being used to stress officer safety issues. The routine begins by ensuring the uniform, body armor, hand-cuffs, duty weapon, shotgun (if used), long gun (if used), tape recorder, chemical agents (if used), impact weapon, electronic control device (if used), and leather or nylon web gear are all in good repair and operational.

The check should include extra or special equipment you may carry with you, whatever it may be, ensuring it too is in good repair and operational. Extra batteries should be carried in the brief case for electronic equipment and flash-light. If the flashlight is rechargeable, is it fully charged? Is there a charger in the patrol unit to keep it operational for the entire shift? If there is no charger in the patrol unit, do you have a portable charging unit? Do you have it with you?

Most agencies require a safety check of the patrol unit as a matter of routine before an officer goes on patrol. I agree with this. However, I believe an officer should go a step or two beyond this. What I am advocating is more than just checking the unit by looking at it. It is **knowing** the unit. You should know where all the switches are for the lights and support equipment, e.g., radio, siren, PA, emergency lights, spot lights, alley lights, brake light kill switch, trunk release button, fuel pump re-set button, shotgun/long rifle rack release button, etc., etc.

Right now you're probably saying to yourself, "Of course I know where they are at, what's the matter with him? This is redundant." You may be right. However, as a matter of good officer safety practice, my reply is, can you operate all of these things by touch, and not by sight?

In high stress situations, such as responding to a robbery in progress, you don't have the luxury of "looking" for switches and knobs, you must operate the equipment by memory retention and touch. This is what is meant by **knowing** the unit. If you are comfortable in the knowledge your equipment, personal and agency, is in good condition and operable, then, I believe, your mind is clear to address the other problems you're going to be presented with during your tour of duty.

As an aside, in order for you to perform fine and gross motor skills, such as handcuffing, shooting, etc., it is necessary for you to continually repeat your training. In actuality this type of training is referred to as "Rote" training, ergo; muscle and thought memory training. The point is, redundancy and repetition are often good things, and are necessary for retaining proper officer safety skills and tactics under high stress situations.

Along with this line of thought, you should also consider other personal equipment, such as your footwear, what you carry in your pockets, and whether or not to wear gloves.

Footwear: Footwear is an important piece of equipment we don't always think about in relation to tactical situations. What kind of boot or shoe do you wear? Is it comfortable? Are the soles and heals rubber or leather? Do your boots or shoes make noise when you walk, either loud footstep noises or squeaky sole noises? It seems silly to ask these questions, I mean, a-boot-is-a-boot-is-a-boot, right? **Wrong!** When it comes to your safety and well being, the footwear you choose is almost as important as the eyeglasses you may need to see properly. Boots or shoes with leather soles and heels are noisy and dangerous. When worn in wet weather, leather soles and heels soak up water and become slippery and could cause you to fall and injure yourself. Worse yet, this could happen while making contact with a suspect. If you were to fall in this situation, you could easily be seriously injured or killed by a suspect who would take advantage of the situation to avoid being arrested. Footwear should be water resistant, light weight, and quiet with a high traction design sole such as the Vibram® sole that grips in dry and wet conditions.

Pockets: Bulky and unnecessary items carried in your pockets hinder your ability to move in a tactical manner and could prevent you from getting through tight locations. Loose change or keys in the pocket create noise and prevent you from moving in a quiet, tactical manner. Secure change and keys before going on patrol. If keys are not needed they should be left in the locker, or in the unit if they are needed for traffic signals or gates. Change should be left in the locker, or kept in a container in the patrol unit. If you don't wear a key holder with a cover on it, put the unit keys in your off hand pocket, not stuck in the buckle of your utility belt. If you are right handed they would go in your left pocket. If you're left handed they would go in your right pocket. This prevents loss, keeps them quiet, and allows you to move in a more tactical manner knowing you won't lose your keys nor will they give away your position.

Gloves: For those of you who wear gloves while on duty, or only on occasion, you may not fully understand how gloves may affect your performance in stressful situations. If you are going to wear gloves they should be good quality leather, or a NOMEX® pilot's glove, that fits properly to avoid loss of dexterity. Gloves can be an aid to you by protecting your hands from being cut, absorbing blood if you are injured, and in some cases protect against foreign or caustic substances that could harm your skin.

More importantly, if you are going to wear gloves, you should train with them. Too often we use equipment in the field that we haven't really trained with, gloves being one of the best examples of this. You must be comfortable in the knowledge that you can reload your weapon, turn your flashlight on and off, get into your pockets, retain your keys, use a pen or pencil, etc., while wearing gloves. If you have to stop and take off your gloves to do simple tasks, then they aren't worth wearing in the first place.

CHAPTER 2
EQUIPMENT

Importance of Proper Equipment

The possession and use of the proper equipment to search a building successfully is just as important to you as the proper equipment a surgeon needs to successfully perform an operation. We don't normally think about the equipment we may need to safely search a building, regardless of when that search may take place. At a minimum you will need a flashlight (day or night), a small mirror, a portable radio, a folding utility knife, your firearm, a length of rope, and doorstops and/or wooden wedges to aid you in the successful search of a building.

This equipment falls under the category of special equipment, as addressed in Chapter 1. Therefore, the care and maintenance of these items is just as important as your other equipment previously discussed.

The Flashlight

The flashlight carried by most officers is usually a four or five cell "mag-type" light, that can be anywhere from 12" to 17" in length. Unfortunately, most officers associate the term "mag-lite" with a hi-intensity light, when in fact it generally isn't. Even so, it is a good piece of equipment and when used in the proper setting is a valuable tool. However, because of

Photo 2.1 – Flashlights

its size and weight it can be a hazard when it comes to safely searching a building or conducting a tactical maneuver that requires stealth and movement, where space may be cramped or limited, or the flashlight has to be carried for extended lengths of time. The use of the term "mag-lite" in the context just described is not a reference to the brand name "Mag-Lite®."

When choosing a flashlight, you need to be aware of the candlepower it will produce. The following information is based on D-cell battery powered flashlights with standard batteries and light bulb. This will give you some idea of the D-cell flashlight candlepower (CP):

- Two cell—4,000 CP
- Three cell—6,000 CP
- Four cell—8,500 CP
- Five cell—12,000 CP

To be effective for our use, the flashlight should be of the highest intensity possible with a minimum 12,000 CP rating. It is obvious that carrying a flashlight with standard batteries and light bulb does not really provide the type of light we want. When lithium batteries and/or xenon or halogen bulbs are used, the CP of the flashlight increases significantly. Some flashlights can get as high as a 30,000 to 50,000 CP rating when standard batteries and bulbs are replaced with hi-tech batteries and bulbs. A Lumen, which equals one unit of candlepower, is also used to measure the flashlight's intensity, so the higher the Lumens, the brighter the light.

The flashlight should be a push button type, which allows controlled use of the light, and of a size manageable in a tactical situation. 5" to 8" in length is an ideal size for ease of use, maneuverability, and storage. I recommend a high intensity light, such as SURE-FIRE'S® series of tactical flashlights manufactured by Laser Products of Fountain Valley, California. They are small, lightweight, rugged lights, offering a wide variety of light systems for almost any tactical application you may encounter. They range in length from approximately 5" to 10", with the majority of them having the push button on the back of the tube for tactical use. Because of their size and weight, they are easily secured in a pocket or on your utility belt without encumbering your ability to move tactically and, when needed, a quick twist of the tube turns on the light for extended use.

Although these lights are my personal preference, there are many good lighting systems available on the market. The key is for you to choose a lighting system for tactical use that you are comfortable with, not just a light to see with in the dark. The smaller tactical light mentioned above, be it a Sure Fire® or other brand, is commonly referred to as a "tac-light." The tactical use of the flashlight will be discussed more completely in Chapter 7.

The Portable Radio

Communication is an essential element for successful law enforcement operations. Throughout the world, officers learn that communication, tactics, planning, and equipment are the base needs of any law enforcement operation. When an officer is placed in the position of having to search a building, or conduct tactical operations requiring stealth and officer safety, communication and communication systems should not be compromised.

To safely conduct these types of missions, a portable radio with a two-way microphone/receiver (commonly referred to as a transceiver) should be used. The transceiver is positioned just off the shoulder, attached to the epaulet of the uniform shirt or jacket. This allows you to turn your head slightly, or lower your head, to talk directly into the transceiver. It also allows you to hear transmissions more clearly and reduces the need for high volume reception. You should adhere to low audio transmission and reception tactics. This means to talk clearly and concisely in a low voice and keep the volume down to a minimal level that only your fellow officers can hear and understand.

One of the best ways to avoid compromising communication discipline is to use a remote earphone, or jack, to augment the transceiver system. This provides more secure audio transmissions between dispatch, the search team and perimeter team. Depending on the type of radio used, this type of accessory may not be compatible with all radios in use by various agencies. If you carry a radio that can't be modified to accommodate an earphone, or jack, then you must be ever mindful that the radio transmissions you send or receive, might also be heard by the suspects. If your radio can't be modified, it behooves you to devise a common, yet simple communication signal system, such as a series of "clicks." In any case, radio transmissions should be kept to an absolute minimum when engaged in the search or while on perimeter.

NEVER turn off your radio! Even with the radio turned down as low as possible, you can immediately call for help when the excrement hits the fan, without having to fumble around to turn on the radio.

The Firearm

The use of firearms in building searches always raises questions as to what is the best type of weapon to use and who should use it. I believe these are relatively easy questions to answer.

It's simple! The firearm should be the weapon most often used on a day-to-day basis, that being your duty weapon. You already have the weapon with you, and have a safe place to put it (in the holster) if you need to have both hands free. You are already comfortable with the weapon, therefore, it is the easiest weapon for you to use in tactical situations. As simple as it sounds, this principle is rarely adhered to.

The type or caliber of the handgun is not at issue here. What is at issue is that you be proficient with the weapon and know its capabilities and limitations.

Who should carry the weapon in a building search situation? Again, it's simple. All members of the search team carry their weapons drawn and ready, unless the situation dictates otherwise. How to tactically use the handgun will be addressed in Chapter 7.

Another consideration is the use of a shotgun or long rifle, such as a Mini-14, AR-15, M-16 or similar type weapon, for the added "firepower" these weapons may provide.

Most agencies do not advocate the use of a long rifle by patrol officers for building searches. I am in total agreement with this. Without going into over-penetration, ballistics, and training issues, suffice it to say that it takes time and training for you to become proficient in the use of these types of specialty weapons, whether they be used in a building search or for some other tactical purpose. As much as I hate to say this, but say it I must, the average patrol officer generally does not possess the skills necessary to enter and search a building with a long rifle, and for this reason alone, should not carry a long rifle to search a building.

However, most agencies do allow for discretionary choices when it comes to the shotgun. The shotgun is an effective offensive weapon when used in the proper patrol environment. It is an ideal weapon for felony or high risk vehicle stops, perimeter positions, or open area searches.

It is my position that a shotgun is a hindrance and safety hazard when used in a building search by the patrol officer. Shotguns carried in patrol units do not normally have slings attached to them for ease of use in tactical situations. Quite often they have an 18" barrel, with an average overall length of 36", sometimes longer.

Unless the shotgun has a pistol grip stock and sling attached to it, it requires two hands to properly control. The fact that the cover officer is the person who will carry the shotgun is not a justifiable argument for its use. There are many times during the search that, because of tactical considerations, the cover officer may become the search officer. When this happens, what happens with the shotgun? Does it get passed from one officer to the other? I think not!

What happens when the cover officer has to move things to get around them, or assist the search officer in moving things? Should the shotgun be set down while performing these tasks? In all probability you will attempt to hold the shotgun with one hand, while trying to open or move something with the other hand. This presents a safety hazard to the search team because the weapon is not being controlled in the proper manner.

What happens if the cover officer has to put down the weapon to affect some other maneuver? Should it be unloaded and disabled? Should it simply have the round removed from the chamber, put on safety, and then put down? To properly relinquish control of the weapon it must be disabled. This means it's unloaded. The rounds go into the officer's pocket. Depending on the type of shotgun, the barrel is removed, or the tube cap is removed and remains in the officer's possession. Then the weapon can be set down. Now we have another problem, what do you do with the barrel, if that's the only way to disable the weapon? There can be still another problem. Can the shotgun, even though disabled, be used against the search team in an offensive manner if grabbed by the crook? The answer to this is yes. It can be used quite easily as a club.

To further add to these complications, the shotgun's size makes it awkward to move with in a stealth manner. It is easy to bump into things with it, get hung up in tight places, such as doorways, stairwells, hallways, and similar areas that are tight and close, limiting your movement. If you still wish to use a shotgun, weigh its alleged advantage of firepower against its disadvantages of maneuverability and safety before arbitrarily grabbing the shotgun and searching the building because you have "heard" it's the right thing to do.

Not to belabor the point, but these same arguments

apply to the carrying of a long rifle as well. One can see just how complicated things can become when carrying a shotgun or long rifle during a building search. And, once again, as much as I hate to say this, but say it I must, the average patrol officer generally does not possess the skills necessary to enter and search a building with a shotgun, and for this reason alone, should not carry a shotgun to search a building.

My position regarding the use of long rifles and shotguns does not apply to their use by SWAT-teams or other specialized units who train with specialty weapons on a regular basis and have specific assignments for, and use of, those weapons. However, if a patrol officer is trained in the use of the long rifle and/or shotgun in building search and clearing methods, then by all means, the decision is theirs as to what weapon they choose to use. My intent is not to place any limitations on officers to be fully prepared for any contingency when conducting a building search that may require the need and use of additional firepower to successfully complete their mission.

The Mirror

The mirror used by a patrol officer in the search of a building should have a single-side, non-distorting reflective surface. It should be a minimum of 3" x 5" in size, capable of fitting into a uniform pocket. It should have some type of protective coating on it to help prevent breakage and keep the user from cutting themselves on the edges of it. I do not recommend the use of metal survival and/or camping

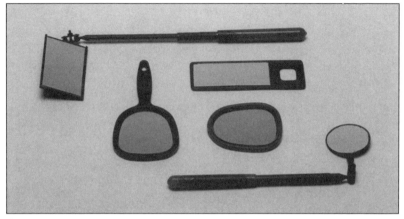

Photo 2.2 – Mirrors

mirrors. The reflective surfaces on these mirrors often distort images at distances greater than 3'. Furthermore, they quite often have two reflective sides, which could compromise the search team by reflecting one or more team member's position when it is being used. The mirror can also be circular in configuration, with a minimum of a 4" diameter. Mirrors may or may not have handles, it doesn't matter. Many officers make their own mirrors to use in tactical situations. As long as you can control the mirror and store it safely when needed, the actual size or diameter is really up to you. Any of the mirrors illustrated in Photo 2.2 are easy to use, however, I would recommend the two extension mirrors, which are mechanics mirrors and provide the most versatility for your use. Regardless of the type of mirror you use, all handles and metal parts should be painted flat black for the obvious reasons. We will discuss the tactical use of mirrors in Chapter 7.

Specialty Tools

Although not normally part of your equipment inventory, these items can be extremely useful when conducting building searches, as well as a variety of other situations you may encounter in the course of your duties. These are small items, easily carried in a briefcase, put into a pocket, taped onto a boot top, or stuffed in the waistband. There are several ways these tools can be used independently or together.

Rope: Rope is used to tie off opposing doors, if necessary, until you are ready to make entry into the secured rooms, and conduct your search. The rope should be 15' to 25' in length with a minimal stretch factor. When I speak of rope, I am referring to parachute cord and household rope. When you cut your parachute cord or rope, be sure to cauterize the ends so they don't unravel. Simply light the ends with a match and let them burn down to a small ball, let it cool, or dip it in water before handling or doing anything else with the ends. I have also found an added measure of insurance, after cauterizing the ends, instead of dipping them in water, I dip them in Plasti Dip,™ a rubberized compound used for tool handles, etc., by doing this I ensure the ends will stay cauterized and not unravel.

Parachute Cord: Parachute cord is quite often the rope of choice because it's lightweight and strong, plus its color is usually a dark OD green or black and doesn't reflect light or stand out if being carried exposed while moving in a stealth manner. It can be purchased at most sporting goods stores

Photo 2.3 – Rope

or military surplus outlets. Parachute cord stretches. This should be considered when tying off a door, or series of doors. The amount of stretch depends on the grade of cord you choose to use. I recommend you test the cord by tying off a door, or a series of doors, and then pull on them to see how far the cord stretches. This will give you a working knowledge of your equipment and may help you decide whether or not to use this method of securing doors in a building search.

Household Rope: I recommend using an all-purpose synthetic rope, commonly used for clotheslines, that is made of polypropylene/polyester blend, that makes it water resistant and easy to work with. I do not recommend rope less than $\frac{3}{16}$" or $\frac{1}{4}$" in diameter. You could use a thicker rope, however

Photo 2.4 – Wedges

it would not be as effective as a thinner rope. The thicker ropes are bulky and cumbersome to carry, and they are awkward to use when tying off knots or loops around small doorknobs or handles. The disadvantage of household rope is the color, which is usually white, making it less than desirable to carry exposed while trying to move in a stealth mode. However, if the rope is not carried openly, it is a good tool to use. And, like parachute cord, this type of rope stretches, therefore, it should be tested before use in an actual situation.

Wedges—Doorstops: Wedges are simple wooden doorstops, varying in size from 1" to 4" in height. They are used to wedge the strike side of the door upwards into the jamb requiring force to open the door. Doors can be wedged inward or outward, although wedging them so the door has to open into the wedge is the most effective. Having more than one wedge allows you to secure more than one door at a time. Training in using wedges on various types of doors should be done to understand their proper use, deployment, and effectiveness.

Wedges are simple to make on a table or radial arm saw from ¾" pine or similar wood. Cut the wedge at a 30° angle. To be stable, the base length should be in proportion to the height. I use a standard size wedge, 2" high tapering down to 5" long. I've found this size is the easiest to carry and will provide the wedging capability needed for almost any type of door. To be "tactical" be sure and paint the wedges flat black so they don't reflect light when carrying them or putting them into use.

Tactical Door Stop: The TACTICAL DOOR STOP™ is a tool designed by Green Company of Hesperia, CA. It is a piece of angle iron, approximately 1½"

Photos 2.5 – 2.6 – Tactical Door Stop™

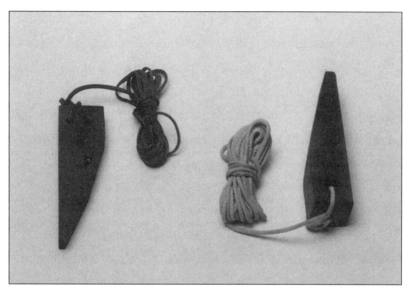

Photo 2.7 – Rope Wedges

in length, slightly rounded, with a hook welded to the back of the angle. It also comes with a belt pouch to carry it in. The hook slides over the hinge of the door between the door-jamb and door; thereby holding the door open wide enough to allow entry, and it will not fall off because of the hooking device. It can be used on all types of doors, from self-closing commercial doors to standard residential type doors. To make this a more effective tactical tool, I have dipped it in Plasti Dip,™ which allows me to place it over the hinge with little or no noise, i.e., metal on metal.

Rope Wedge: This is a universal tool combining the rope and wedge together into a tool I call the "rope wedge." This is made from a piece of 2" x 2" pine, or similar wood. The wedge should be an average of 6" to 8" in length, with a

30° angle for the wedge. A hole is centered and drilled 1" from the back of the wedge large enough to accept the parachute cord or rope you have chosen to use. The parachute cord or rope should be 15' to 25' in length. Loop one end of the parachute cord or rope through the hole in the wedge, make the loop large enough to allow it to be moved up or down or sideways, then tie it off with a square knot. If you don't leave the loop large enough to move, you will find it difficult to pull the wedge loose from under the door when you are positioned at an angle away from the door. The wedge can be made from narrower stock as well. The purpose of the thicker stock is to eliminate the chance of breaking the wedge when pulling on it with the rope. You can also use this tool to tie off doors if they can't be wedged closed. The officer safety factor of this tool is that the rope allows you to remove the wedge from the door at a safe distance. Again, be sure and paint the wedges a flat black.

Knife: Generally knives are not considered a law enforcement tool, however, they should be. Knives can be used for a variety of things in your normal day-to-day duties. One public safety use would be to cut seat belts at the scene of an accident. The type of knife an officer carries is usually one of personal choice. I would suggest you use a folding type knife of good quality, one that will hold a good cutting edge and is strong and durable under pressure, such as in a prying motion. This type of knife can be carried on your utility belt

Photo 2.8 – Knives and Multi-Tools

in a holder as a part of your normal equipment, in your pocket, or clipped on your pants waistband or pocket.

In a building search, the knife can be used to cut through screens, pry open aluminum screen doors, pry open windows, and cut open packages suspected of containing evidence or contraband (as long as the law permits it). It can be used as a screwdriver, or to hold open doors and windows in emergency situations. In reality, how you use a knife tactically is limited only by your imagination. You may opt to carry a "multi-tool" such as the "Leatherman Tool™," which combines a knife with a variety of useful tools, such as pliers, light duty wire snips, a saw, punch, etc. A word of caution, before carrying either of these tools, be sure you're not violating agency policy.

Other Tools For Consideration

What you carry with you, or what is available to you is of importance. Not only do you carry your primary weapon, but you carry a variety of other "tools of the trade." Aside from the weapon, three of these tools are important and must be remembered when conducting building searches and suspect contacts.

First are the handcuffs: Each member of the search team should carry at least two sets of handcuffs and as many sets of flex cuffs as is convenient. It is highly unlikely you will encounter multiple suspects inside a building, but you must be prepared for this possibility. As an additional tactical tool, handcuffs, and flex-cuffs, can be used to secure doors in the open or closed position, such as French doors or commercial exit doors.

Second are leg irons: Each member of the search team should also carry two sets of leg irons. They are easily carried in the rear pocket of the uniform pants, or in a jacket pocket that keeps them from rattling so as to maintain proper noise discipline. There is always the possibility a suspect's wrists may be too large for standard handcuffs, thus requiring the use of leg irons to safely secure them. Like handcuffs, leg irons can be used to secure doors.

> NOTE: As a matter of routine, I do not recommend using handcuffs, flex-cuffs, or leg irons as "tie off" tools. I mention these facts as one more means of using tools at your disposal when circumstances dictate the need to do something unusual with something unusual.

Third is the baton: The baton is probably the most over-looked and forgotten tool we have. More often than not it is left in the patrol unit. Generally it is left behind because of the belief it is more of a hindrance than an asset, or you are uncomfortable carrying it and using it.

It doesn't matter if it is a straight baton, ASP® or side-handle baton, it can be used tactically in a building search. The obvious reason for carrying the baton is to negate the use of deadly force if the suspect resists and the situation calls for the use of an impact weapon. The not so obvious, is using the baton tactically when entering and searching a building.

There is a tactical way to carry the baton during a building search. Insert it inside your waistband at the small of your back; placing it far enough down inside your pants to ensure that it will not fall out. If it is a side-handle baton, place the handle flat against your back, to the right or left side, depending on which hand you will use to retrieve it.

Photo 2.9 – Baton Carry – Standing   Photo 2.10 – Baton Carry – Kneeling

This carrying method allows for immediate retrieval of the baton when it's needed. The carrying method is not uncomfortable and does not limit or hinder your movements. Carrying the baton in this manner, and not in the baton ring or holder, keeps it from banging against objects, thus allowing for stealth movement.

Photo 2.11 – Off-hand baton retrieval

However, you must always be cautious when carrying the baton and moving about with it. Even though it is tucked away to prevent it from swinging about, the baton will protrude outward and present a high profile when bending over or stooping down, allowing it to strike against objects or walls that it would not normally strike if you were in the standing position.

If you don't have a doorstop or wedge, the baton can be used to prop open self-closing doors. By placing the baton between the door and the doorjamb, on the hinge side, let the door close against it. This will effectively keep the door open without any physical effort on your part. It can also be wedged under commercial doors to prop them open, or keep them closed. Normally, these types of doors have a much wider space between the door bottom and floor than do doors in residential dwellings.

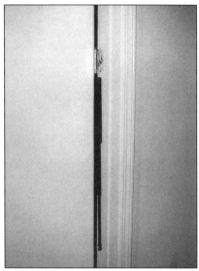

Photo 2.12 – Baton used as a door wedge

Photo 2.13 – ASP™ used as a door wedge

The baton can be used to search with as well. You can use it to clear under beds, rake across closet shelves or other potential hiding places that you may not be able to see or reach. It can be used to penetrate clothing inside of closets, or piles of clothing, to ensure that a suspect isn't concealed within hanging or piled clothing. How you use the baton in a tactical manner is up to your imagination. However, always be conscious of the probability of a suspect grabbing it if you

Photo 2.14 – ASP™ Carry – Standing

Photo 2.15 – ASP™ Carry – Kneeling   Photo 2.16 – ASP™ Off-hand retrieval

strike them with it in a search mode, always be prepared to react to this potentiality.

If you carry the ASP® it should be extended (opened) prior to entering the building and carried in the same tactical manner as described earlier, and collapsed only after you have left the building and no longer need it.

Useful Items Inside the Building

How many times have officers searched a building, needed something with which to open a door or wedge a door closed, and not have anything with them to do it? Probably more times than any of us care to admit. Often times, no thought is given to the things inside a building, which can help us make our search easier and safer.

A few examples of these items are mops and brooms, to push open doors and/or wedge them open, or wedge them closed. Mirrors inside rooms can be looked into at angles before entering the room, checking to see if someone is hiding behind a door, or in a blind corner. Chairs or stepladders can be used to stand on to look on top of bookcases, shelves, closets, high cupboards, etc. These are only a few of the more obvious things. The list can go on-and-on. It is recommended these considerations be a part of the overall tactical plan where you are consciously thinking about what could be used to help make your search safer and more efficient.

CHAPTER 3
THE CALL

Crime-in-Progress

When a crime-in-progress call, such as a burglary or robbery is dispatched, the end result usually generates some type of a search for suspects, either a building search or an area search. When you receive these types of calls you should immediately begin thinking about possible routes of escape and/or evasion tactics the suspects may use. You should already have some formulation of a plan of action as to what route of travel you are going to take to the call, where you want the back-up units positioned, and where you will position your own unit when you arrive at the call scene.

The plan must have a definitive method to block escape routes and contain the area. The only way to properly be able to do these things is for you to have a sound, working knowledge of your beat and a good working knowledge of the surrounding beats to know from where your assistance will be responding.

There are five basic tactics officers commonly overlook when responding to calls of a crime-in-progress:

1. Taking time to check for suspicious persons or vehicles in the general vicinity of the call.

2. Taking time to check for suspicious persons or vehicles around the immediate area of the primary location.

3. Taking time to check for suspicious persons or vehicles leaving the immediate area of the call.

4. Talking with witnesses or other persons who may be able to describe suspects and/or give other intelligence information about the building or area to be searched.

5. Establishing an inner perimeter in a timely manner around the primary location to block potential avenues of escape.

Communication Between Responding Units

What I am going to tell you next you already know. However, in order to raise your awareness level regarding the importance of communication, I feel it important to re-emphasize the process.

The dispatcher starts the communication process by transmitting the call to the primary and back-up officers. It is the primary officer's responsibility to respond directly to the call to gather crime, suspect, and victim information. This officer is responsible for telling dispatch where to place back-up units, or personally direct the back-up units into positions to block escape routes and establish a perimeter around the area of the call.

To re-emphasize a point made earlier, the primary officer must have a plan of action to direct other units into the area to establish a perimeter. The primary officer must gather the needed information about the crime and communicate it accurately to the assisting officers, dispatch, and the supervisor.

As back-up units are responding, they should give dispatch the locations from where they are responding. Generally, this type of notification is done to ensure the closest units are used most effectively if it doesn't interfere with the exigent circumstance of the call and the ability to safely dispatch the primary unit. To effectively set up a containment perimeter, the primary and back-up units must communicate with each other as they move into the area of the call. This prevents them from "over-running" each other's position while they are sealing off the area.

A major problem in establishing effective communication is the "air time" it takes to coordinate the responding units. If only two or three units are responding, generally, the problem is not too great. However, when four or more units respond, this complicates the communication problem because of the number of officers involved. The simplest method to avoid "over-talking" from the uninvolved units, and to avoid confusion created by too many people on the air, is for the responding units to use a tactical frequency. This does not interfere with the primary frequency of the agency, and permits car-to-car communication, thus making it easier to set up the perimeter and communicate pertinent information between the responding units, the supervisor, and dispatch.

If tactical frequencies are not available, the primary officer should request a clear channel. Once the units are in place, and satisfactory control of the situation has been established, the clear channel status can be lifted. Car-to-car communication is done using a clear channel for the same reason you would use a tactical channel.

Checking For Suspects While Responding

As you approach the call, routes of travel leading into the location of the call are visually checked. The immediate vicinity surrounding the call must be checked as well. These visual searches are accomplished in three ways:

1. By the primary units
2. By the back-up units
3. With air support

Primary Unit Responsibility: If you are the primary unit arriving at the scene, you should be looking for suspicious vehicles and persons who may be leaving the area. Be aware of persons who are running, walking fast or extremely slow, or appear to be evading or hiding from you as you approach. You should also be looking for vehicles leaving the area at an unusually high speed, or an unusually low speed, or appear to be taking evasive action as you make your approach. And be aware of, and suspicious of, persons who may be lingering in the area of the call or whose actions are extraordinary in appearance to you. These persons could easily be look-outs, a possible ambush, or some other type of accomplice in the crime to which you are responding or, they could even be the suspect.

If you, as a primary officer, locate a possible suspect while en route to the call, you should detain them and remain with the alleged suspect until information is developed that either links the person to the crime or eliminates their involvement. In so doing, you would relinquish your status as primary unit to a back-up unit which would then become the primary unit.

Back-up Unit Responsibility: Back-up units should take avenues of approach that are likely escape routes for suspects. Back-up units should also check for the behavioral patterns previously mentioned, however, they have the luxury of being able to more closely scrutinize people and vehicles. Since they are not the initial responders, back-up units can slow their response to match their search and containment maneuvers. In effect, they are establishing a "roving perimeter." Once information is received from the primary units about the type of crime, suspect, vehicle description, directions of travel, etc., the back-up units will seal off the area by setting a static perimeter.

Air Support Responsibility: Air support is used during the initial phases of the call. The helicopter should not respond to the primary scene, unless extenuating circumstances regarding the safety of a citizen or officer dictate. By remaining a tactical distance away from the primary location, the noise from the helicopter will not alert suspects to the presence of other responding units.

The helicopter is used to conduct grid searches around

the primary location looking for the same suspect traits described above until called into the scene by the primary units. Once called to the scene, the helicopter conducts a visual check of high ground locations, rooftops, etc., and the immediate area around the location for possible suspects and vehicles the ground units may not be able to see. Once the air search is completed the helicopter leaves the area until needed again.

Suspects In The Immediate Area Of The Call: As an issue of officer safety to the primary officer, and eventually the search team, and containment personnel, the immediate area surrounding the primary location must be visually and physically searched before conducting the entry and search of the building. It is not uncommon for suspects to hide within the immediate area of the crime they have just committed or attempted to commit. Often times these individuals have police scanners to monitor radio calls, and may have cell phones or radios of their own to communicate with their crime partners, whether the crime partners are inside or outside the building. All officers responding to the scene should be aware of these facts. The primary officers on the scene should be acutely aware of these possibilities as they begin to establish the inner perimeter.

Inner Perimeter Area Search: Once the inner perimeter is set, a thorough search for suspects in the surrounding area is conducted. This is done by two officers, as with the search of the building, one officer will search while the other covers.

Again, you should remember the possibility of a lookout. The search team should move slowly and deliberately when approaching likely areas of suspect concealment or cover. Remember to **stop, look, and listen frequently** as you move about during the search and before making visual or physical contact with possible areas of suspect concealment or cover.

Some of the locations and items to be searched are large and small trash cans, rooftops (if not already checked by air support) bushes, trees, under and inside vehicles, doorways of adjoining or nearby buildings, piles of materials such as wood and brick, or other locations where a person is likely to conceal themselves.

Officer Safety Reminder
"Winning isn't everything, it's the only thing"
—Vince Lombardi

As we all know, Coach Lombardi made this statement in one of his famous halftime speeches to motivate his team to victory in a GAME of football. I used this quote for two reasons: First I do believe that winning is a very important part of our daily lives, even though, try as we may, we don't always win. However, we should never stop, or give up and must always strive to win in all that we do in life, be it raising a family, participating in competitive sports, in business, etc., etc. Second, and most importantly, our profession is NOT A GAME, and winning IS the only thing. There are no second place winners in a fight for your life or a deadly force confrontation. Read that last sentence again to be sure you understand what is meant by, "no second place winners." If you don't understand it, what it means is, you may survive the encounter, but end up severely wounded, forced to retire, or worse yet, in a coma or a paraplegic for the rest of your life. That IS NOT winning, that's simply surviving. That's why I don't use the word "survival," and believe, without reservation, that WINNING is the only option we have. Yes, we do have rules to govern our conduct and actions. However, you must be prepared to do whatever it takes for you to win and go home at the end of your shift. This attitude and commitment you most definitely owe to your fellow officers, but most importantly you owe it to yourself and your family.

I recently read the book, *We Were Soldiers Once—And Young,* the story of Lt. Gen. Hal G. Moore, USA (Ret) and the Battle of the Ia Drang Valley, Vietnam, November 1965, which was, in essence, the start of the Vietnam War. What most people don't know is that this battle was the epitome of fighting and winning against overwhelming odds. The Americans had 428 soldiers, 29 officers, while the NVA had over 3,000 troops. The Americans won a decisive victory.

Years later, when asked about that battle, the General was quoted as saying, "One important lesson is that training and dogged determination, tenacity and willpower can turn the tide of a battle. In the battle, a couple of times it was really, really close, but never once did it cross my mind that we would go down. I have always had the precept that if you think you might lose; you have already lost in whatever enterprise you are involved in. I just knew we would prevail."[1] What better way to get across to you the importance of having and maintaining a winning mindset?

It is important for you to understand that crooks train too. Maybe not the same way we do, but they learn from us by watching how we do things so they can counter what we do so they can commit their criminal acts. To help you win in this potentially deadly game, you need to develop the same knowledge and understanding of the criminal as the criminal has of you. An important part of that knowledge is trying to place yourself in the mindset of the suspect, i.e., try to think like the suspect and, as strange as it may sound, move like the suspect. If you believe you can see the suspect when you arrive at the scene, or while setting up perimeters, then in all probability the suspect has already seen you, therefore you must move in a manner that lessens this possibility, ergo, moving like a suspect would move in their attempt to avoid being seen by you.

If you would remember this, we could lessen the possibilities of escalating an incident into a barricaded subject, barricaded/hostage situation, or worse yet, causing an officer or citizen to get injured or killed. To paraphrase a cliché, "always look for the unusual and expect the unexpected."

[1]Armchair General, September 2004

CHAPTER 4
PERIMETERS

Inner and Outer Perimeters

Perimeters are established for four reasons at crime-in-progress calls or calls where a building or area search is obvious.

1. Prevent escape by the suspects

2. Contain and control the situation

3. Keep unauthorized persons out of the area of operation

4. Provide staging areas for additional manpower and materials if needed

The accepted terms used in law enforcement for perimeters are "inner perimeter" and "outer perimeter." Another term often heard in law enforcement is "containment." To contain an objective is the same as setting a perimeter, therefore, containment and perimeter are generally synonymous with each other in law enforcement circles.

Officers, by their very nature, want to be close to the action when things start to happen. Unfortunately, when it comes to building searches and setting perimeters, this desire often is a detriment rather than an attribute.

The Inner Perimeter

The inner perimeter is set around the primary building at a safe distance from the building to block avenues of escape, contain the suspects, and provide immediate access to suspects for a safe, speedy arrest. The inner perimeter should be set as soon as tactically possible.

The inner perimeter officers act as an immediate arrest team in the event suspects exit the building without warning, or at the direction of the officers. They also provide security for the search team when the time comes for them to make entry and conduct the search. These added responsibilities require the inner perimeter officers to remain alert and aware of their environment. They should also pay close attention to communication between search team members, as well as communication from the search team to the perimeter teams. It is the responsibility of the inner perimeter officers to report to the search team any noises or other unusual activities they may hear or see from their positions.

Closer is not always better: This is a good rule to remember when selecting your position on the inner perimeter. By setting up too close, your line-of-sight and field-of-vision into and around the building are limited and your reaction time is reduced significantly if a suspect leaves the building unexpectedly. Being too close also drastically reduces the field-of-fire for covering the search team. Moreover, taking a position in an area or location that may be exposed to the suspect's vision and/or field-of-fire jeopardizes your personal safety. However, being too far away limits your ability to control exiting suspects, and detect movement or noise inside the building. Of course the situation will dictate where and how you set the inner perimeter, but keeping these principles in mind should help you select the proper tactical position.

"Cornering" or "Diagonal" Perimeter of a Building: In most cases an effective inner perimeter can be established by two officers "cornering" the building or setting a "diagonal" watch down two sides of a building. However, there are two major problems with this tactic.

1. Officer safety is jeopardized because there is no line of sight between the two officers, lending it to crossfire situations that are almost unavoidable.

2. It is a rigid tactic that does not allow for change when needed. If the officer remembers to think about what the suspect sees, not what the officer can see, it may cause the officer to change his position on the perimeter.

The following two illustrations depict diagonal cornering tactics using two officers, and four officers. Illustration 1 shows two officers with dual areas of responsibility. Illustration 2 shows four officers each with a single area of responsibility.

In Illustration 1, if you draw an imaginary line down the sides of the building to the right and left of each officer, you can see that each officer has dual areas of responsibility. This creates an officer safety problem because the officers do not have visual or auditory contact with each other.

Furthermore, the officer's observation capabilities are diminished because they may be forced to look from one side to the other based on the building's configuration. In so doing the officers may miss seeing a suspect moving about or exiting the building in an attempt to escape. The stationary positions of the officers show how rigid this tactic can be.

Based on manpower availability, this may be the only inner perimeter tactic available. When faced with the decision to use it, do so with the knowledge of its limitations and officer safety issues and, as stated many times by many people, there are no 100% safe ways to do our jobs.

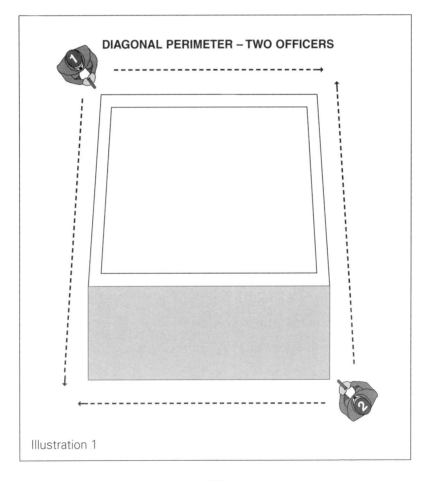

DIAGONAL PERIMETER – TWO OFFICERS

Illustration 1

Illustration 2 depicts how much safer it is to use four officers to corner a building. Draw an imaginary line down each side of the building away from each officer and you will see that each officer has only one area of responsibility and can maintain visual and auditory contact with a partner. By placing two officers on one corner, you now have proper control of the inner perimeter to observe movement and block potential escape routes.

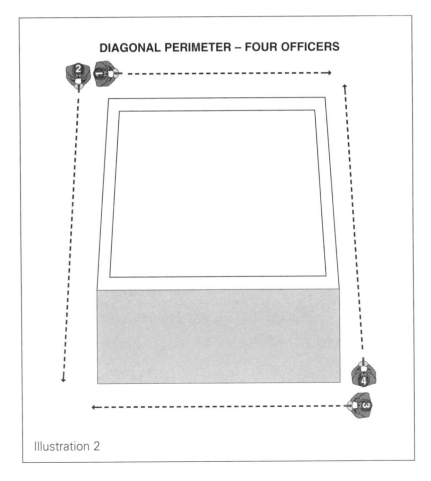

DIAGONAL PERIMETER – FOUR OFFICERS

Illustration 2

I recommend this tactic when manpower permits. It provides exceptional observation capabilities, regardless of the building's configuration, and conforms to the officer safety aspects of the partner principle, while minimizing crossfire situations. Just a side note about "crossfire situations." I don't believe we will ever eliminate crossfire situations, no matter how good our tactics become. That's why I think it's more accurate to use the terminology of minimizing so it doesn't give the false belief you can eliminate this danger.

If there are only two officers available to set the inner perimeter, then other factors regarding how to use the "cornering" or "diagonal" perimeter method should be considered. For example, if there is a lack of obvious escape ports, such as doors or windows, on a particular side of a building, then there is no need to place an officer on a corner or diagonal that encompasses that side of the building as a part of a static perimeter. This would allow the two officers to work as partner officers and/or provide additional manpower for other needs if one officer can safely secure the perimeter.

The Outer Perimeter

Generally, outer perimeters are a luxury when it comes to a patrol situation involving the search of a building. They are normally used in more dangerous situations, such as an armed/barricaded subject, ambushes, sniper incidents, etc. In any case, it is important for you to know and understand the purpose of an outer perimeter, and how one is established.

The outer perimeter is established around the primary area of operations within which the inner perimeter is set. It could be a city block, a single street, one or two houses or buildings around the primary location, or whatever it takes to allow for a safe area of operation for the officers involved in the incident and the general public.

Static control points are set on the outer perimeter. These control points limit the ingress and egress of personnel and should be set at a location, or locations, away from a direct line of vision to the operation. When possible, only one control point should be used. The actual perimeter area is secured by additional personnel spaced tactically around the entire perimeter to keep out unauthorized personnel. The primary purpose of control points is to avoid interference with the tactical operations by unauthorized persons.

When establishing the outer perimeter, you must consider the suspect's line-of-vision in relation to your positions on the perimeter. If the suspects are armed, consider the effective range of their weapons and their fields-of-fire.

Manpower and equipment needs have to be considered when deciding on establishing an outer perimeter. More officers are needed to establish and maintain the outer perimeter than the inner perimeter.

If you are assigned outer perimeter responsibilities you must guard against becoming too relaxed or complacent because you believe you are removed from the primary area of operations. You must be vigilant to persons who show an undue interest in what is going on by asking unusual questions or displaying an unusual amount of knowledge of the situation. Persons of this nature could be additional suspects or accomplices.

The single, most important question you need to ask is, "Does the perimeter distance establish a safe, effective buffer zone for the protection of the operation and the public?" It is easier to set an outer perimeter larger than necessary when first gaining control over the situation. Doing this ensures containment within the perimeter of possible evidence, and controlling the buildings, which could be used tactically by the officers handling the situation. It is easier to shrink the outer perimeter than to expand it once it is established.

Operations Positions: The outer perimeter permits setting up strategic locations for the Command Post, Tactical Command Post, Staging Area, and Negotiators Command Post within the outer perimeter, yet out of the line-of-vision of the primary area of operation.

A location for the Media Command Post is secured outside the outer perimeter away from the area of actual operations, and out of the line-of-vision and sight of the primary area of operation.

Invisible Deployment: Whether on foot or in the patrol unit, silence should be one of your primary considerations when arriving at the location and setting up the perimeter. Invisible deployment means no more than moving in a tactical manner, using proper cover, concealment, movement tactics, and noise discipline. This keeps you from being detected by the suspect or being silhouetted by light, which would allow the suspect to locate you.

Movement or Changing Positions: In theory, the only time you need move is to better block escape routes, or take a better cover position. Any time you change position, the other perimeter team members must be alerted to where and when you are moving. Before moving, you must select where you are going to move to, then take a route of travel out of the line-of-sight of the suspect. If a diversion is needed to cover your movement, be sure it is directed away from the location you came from, and away from your route of travel to the location to which you are moving. If you have to move or change your position, use proper cover, concealment and movement tactics. Don't become complacent simply because you believe your current position is not visible to the suspect, or you feel your present position is not very important. Remember, if it weren't necessary for you to be in this position, you wouldn't be there in the first place, so stay put, unless it's a safety issue.

CHAPTER 5
THE TACTICAL PLAN

"A journey of a thousand miles must begin with a single step"
—Lao-Tzu - Tao Te Ching

Pre-Entry Planning

Before making entry into the building a tactical plan of action must be determined. The search and perimeter personnel should be involved in establishing the tactical plan of action. Remember to KISS it! As stated before, my KISS principle is to: "Keep It Safe and Simple."

Some important considerations when making a tactical plan are:

- Is there a suspect description?
- Is the suspect armed?
- Are there witnesses?
- Is a floor plan available?
- Are keys available to use?
- Is a responsible person available to come to the scene?
- Where and how will the search team enter?
- Who will enter first?
- Who will cover?
- Who will search?
- What direction will the search team go once inside the building?

Other important points in formulating your tactical plan include:

- What tactics are needed?
- Should a canine team be used first, or in conjunction with the two man search team?
- What communications will the search team use once inside the building?
- What if a suspect is found?
- Who will be the search and control officer?
- Who will remove the suspect from the building?
- Are there sufficient perimeter personnel to take control of a suspect?
- Can one team effectively search the building?
- Are more teams needed?
- Are there animals or other hazards inside?
- What are the lighting conditions?
- Should demands for surrender be made, etc., etc., etc.

These are some of the most obvious questions and important points the search team and perimeter personnel should consider when putting together their entry and search plans. What can you add to these lists?

And of course, the major factor to consider when formulating the tactical plan is the number of officers available to assist. If additional officers are available, consideration should be given to setting up a three or four person search team. The additional officers function as cover officers until a suspect is located, at which time they become the control and arrest officers. They would give the commands to the suspect, conduct the search and handcuffing, and remove the suspect from the building.

The Tactical Plan

Entry Team: The first phase of the tactical plan addresses entering the building. Before this can be done, it must be decided who will be on the entry team. The entry team must establish an entry point and what method of entry will be used to gain access into the building. Who will search? Who will cover? Who will clear the entry point? Will both officers go in together? Will one officer enter and dominate the room first or will one officer dominate the room with their weapon from the outside while the other officer enters?

If there are more than two officers on the team, when will the additional officers enter, after the primary search team enters, or at the same time the primary search team enters? Regardless of what the tactical plan is, the primary considerations are always officer safety, communication, speed, silence, and silhouetting. Patrol officers should never use dual, or multiple entry points and teams.

Speed vs. Officer Safety: Speed is never substituted for officer safety. Speed is essential when moving from one point of cover or concealment to another, or when going through openings, crossing unusually large open spaces such as open warehouse bays, a yard, a street, or similar expanses. Openings are cleared quickly and quietly to avoid silhouetting.

A strong word of caution! Do not confuse speed of entry with speed of search. Never compromise officer safety by speeding up the search effort because you believe the time you have to search the building is limited. Time, for all practical purposes is always on your side when conducting a building search. When a search is rushed, suspects are not found, and officer safety is compromised because proper search techniques are not followed, and that could result in injury or death to you and/or your partner.

Stealth Search: Oftentimes the term "stealth" and "invisible deployment" are only used in conjunction with SWAT-teams. There is no reason why these terms and their application should not be adopted by patrol officers. They are simple terms describing audio nuance (silence) and physical movement (stealth or invisible deployment) by all members of the team. By moving in a stealth mode, utilizing cover and concealment, search team members do not compromise themselves to suspects as they move through the building. The team is better able to hear the suspect's movements over their own. Less energy is required to complete the search because the team's movements are slow and deliberate. To maintain a proper stealth mode, the search team should use hand signals when possible. Radio discipline is a must when staging to make entry and, once inside the building, radio traffic should be kept to an absolute minimum.

CHAPTER 6
ENTRY AND MOVEMENT

"One must learn by doing the thing; though you think you know it, you have no certainty until you try."
—Sophocles, Trachimiae

Clearing and Entry Tactics

Clearing Tactics: There are three basic methods used to clear a room or area, prior to a search team making an entry. They are used to clear doorways, windows, hallways, stairways, or other entry points, openings, or areas. Clearing simply means you are attempting to make your entry as safe as possible by identifying possible suspects and obstacles, such as furniture, or other safety hazards such as doorways, closets, stairways, half-walls, etc., within the room or area you intend to enter. These methods are:

1. Slicing-the-pie
2. Mirroring
3. Quick Peek

Any of these methods, or a combination of them should be used by the search team as they move through a building.

Types of Entry Tactics: Once the entry point is cleared, there are three basic tactical maneuvers, which can be used to gain access into the building, room, or area.

1. The Crossing Pattern—"X" Pattern
2. The Line Entry—Diagonal
3. The Buttonhook—Wrap Around

Any of these maneuvers, or a combination of them, should be used to enter rooms inside the building as the search team conducts their search. The room to be entered is divided into sections, or halves. Each officer has his section, or half as his Area Of Responsibility (AOR).

Clearing Points of Entry

Slicing-The-Pie: This method uses minutes-of-angle, commonly referred to as "slicing-the-pie" or "fanning" to clear an area or opening. It can be used to clear doorways, hallways,

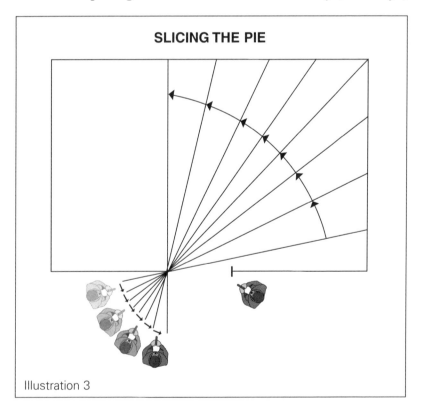

SLICING THE PIE

Illustration 3

windows, stairwells, or other entry points that are at eye level. Although a good tactic, it has limited observation capabilities. The ability to see inside the area being cleared is diminished because of distance, lighting conditions, and confinement of space available to move.

To use this technique, one officer slices-the-pie, while the other officer covers the door opening. It is important to understand the correct position from which to slice-the-pie. Using the doorway and the wall as concealment, the clearing officer draws an imaginary line at a 90° angle outward from the edge of the doorway, to a distance great enough to allow movement to the imaginary line, yet not so great that he becomes exposed to the suspect's line of vision. But not so limited that once the limitation point has been reached, the officer cannot safely and adequately see inside the opening.

By using short deliberate steps, you move at a 45° angle parallel to the doorway. As you are moving, your attention is focused on the area inside the doorway, identifying what you see. This movement continues until you are parallel with the edge of the doorway, which should place you at or near the end of your imaginary line.

As the clearing officer, hold your weapon in the master grip in a combat stance, directing it at the doorway that is being cleared. The cover officer is positioned slightly back from the doorway, facing inward at an angle allowing him to focus his attention on what may be inside the doorway from where the clearing officer is moving while "slicing-the-pie."

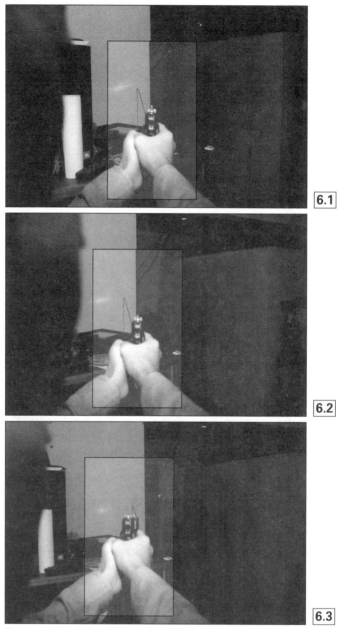

6.1

6.2

6.3

Photos 6.1 – 6.6 – Slicing the Pie

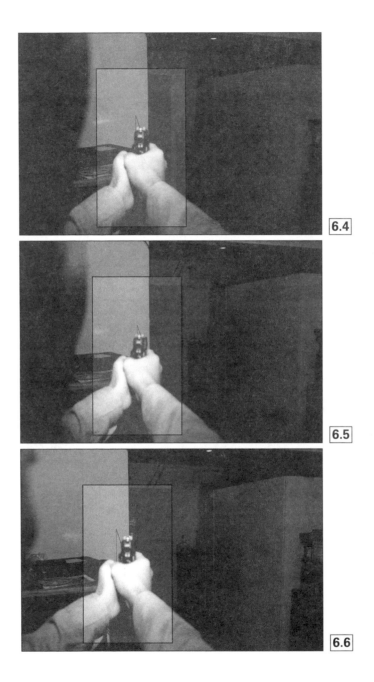

6.4

6.5

6.6

When one side is cleared, the opposite side should then be cleared. Each side should be cleared by the officer located on that side. In other words, if you're on the right side of the opening, you clear from the right side. Conversely, if you're on the left side, then you clear that side. The same officer can clear both sides, however it is generally safer, and easier, to switch roles at this point. The cover officer becomes the clearing officer, remaining in position while the clearing officer becomes the covering officer.

Once both sides of the entry have been cleared, if it becomes necessary to re-evaluate the entry plans because of what one, or both of the officers may have seen, then move away from the entry point and do so before entering the building.

Mirroring: If a mirror can be used to clear the entry point, or other unknown areas, then by all means use it. To clear the entry point, mirror from the center of the doorway outward to the front, inside corners (the deadly corners) of the room. If the area to be mirrored is a window or similar type opening, mirror at the bottom front corners (the corners directly right and left of the window) first, then move inward and clear the area below the window or opening, then outward to the back inner corners of the room. As one officer mirrors, the other officer covers the point of entry. If the area being mirrored is a doorway, mirror from a position lower or higher than normal.

Quick Peeking: Quick peeking is exactly what the term implies, a method by which an officer quickly "peeks" or looks around a corner, door opening, or window to see what is present in the area he is looking into. The quick peek is done by taking a position either high or low behind the cover or concealment of the opening or corner. You then "quickly" peek around your position of cover or concealment to identify what is in the area you are preparing to move to. You should only expose half of your head to do this, and no longer than one or two seconds.

The obvious problem with this tactic is exposing yourself to possible attack, especially if you have not had the advantage of clearing any part of the room with either a mirror or by slicing-the-pie prior to quick peeking into an area. It would be easy for a suspect to be directly behind or beside the area you are going to quick peek into, thereby subjecting you to the attack previously mentioned. For this reason alone, I do not care to use the quick peek technique. The other reason I don't care to use it is because it is difficult to acclimate your eye and head movement effectively; so that you actually see something in the area you are quick peeking into. If you do wish to use this method, as always, train and practice before applying it to a real situation.

Doorways: Before entering a building or room through a doorway, clear the hinge side first by gently pushing the door open until it strikes the wall or stops. Look between the hinge side of the door and the doorjamb to ensure that no one is hiding behind it. By pushing the door open gently, you avoid alerting the suspects that the search team is entering the building. If the door stops sooner than you believe it should, there is a good possibility someone may be hiding behind it. Suspects still hide behind doors! Don't be foolish and forget to check behind the door.

If it's too dark to see safely between the jamb and door, the area can be lit by placing the flashlight on the floor, or ground, or squat down and direct the beam under the door at an angle towards the corner into which the door opens. This method can be used in daylight or darkness, but be careful not to silhouette yourself or your partner when you are squatting down, putting down the flashlight, or retrieving it. Do not shine the light through the door space at eye level, it gives away your position, and can temporarily blind you and/or take away your night vision capabilities.

Photos 6.7 – 6.8 – Opening doors

The officer on the opposite side of the door cautiously looks between the door and doorjamb for the shape or shadow of a person. If this officer can't see through the opening, then the officer on the hinge side should clear it. This can be accomplished in one of four ways. You can "quick peek," use a mirror, squat, or lie down to see through the opening. Regardless of which method you use, remember to look through the opening from a position not expected by the suspect, and **NEVER** look from the same location twice.

Windows: A window, or similar type opening, presents unique clearing and entry problems. If the team has to climb through a window, the corners directly below the window are cleared first. Next, clear inward towards the center of the window or opening, checking directly below the area into which the team will be climbing.

This is done for two reasons:

1. To locate hidden suspects either in the front corners of the room, or directly below, or inside, the window or opening.

2. To look for and identify obstacles that may hinder or prevent the team from making a safe entry.

When making a window entry, the search team should use a ladder or similar device. This adds to the overall safety of the entry by elevating the team to a point of advantage to climb over a window sill, or opening edge. Only one officer can enter at a time with this method. As the first officer enters, the second officer covers the opening, focusing his attention into the area the first officer is entering. Once inside, the first officer takes a low combat stance, moving away from the opening, being careful not to silhouette himself, and dominates the room with his weapon. He directs his attention to any location from where a potential threat may emanate, while the second officer makes his entry.

Clearing Reminders: This may seem redundant, however, it's worth emphasizing again that all of the clearing methods described above are done for the following reasons:

- To locate hidden suspects either behind furniture, in the corners of the room, or directly below, or inside the window opening.

- To look for and identify obstacles that may hinder or prevent the team from making a safe entry into the room or area.

- To determine if both entry team members can enter the room together to dominate and search the room.

- To determine if only one member can enter the room, as the other member dominates the room with his weapon, while his partner makes entry and searches the room.

If the location of the doorway, or other entry point, only allows approach by one officer, the cover officer should take a position at an angle behind the clearing officer, which allows a clear field-of-fire and line-of-vision into the area to be cleared. Generally, this doesn't change the type of clearing methods the officer chooses to use.

The Danger Areas: Regardless of the type of clearing and entry methods used, there are two primary danger areas you must know about in order to clear and dominate a room as safely as possible. First, are the inside front corners of a room that are often referred to as the "deadly corners" or "hard corners" because these are the most difficult to clear by the search team.

The second danger is the doorway or opening that you will be going through, and includes the immediate area inside the doorway or opening, and extending to the back

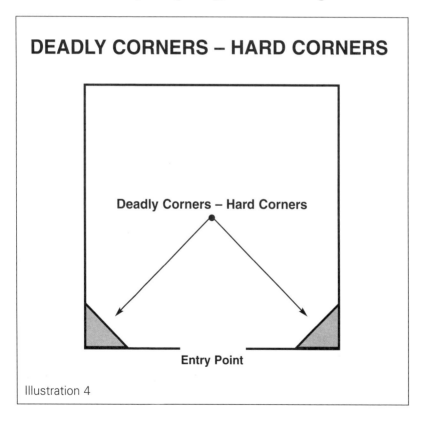

Illustration 4

wall of the room, or the deepest part of an area, that you are making entry into. This area is commonly referred to as the "fatal funnel." It is in the "fatal funnel" that you become a target! You are most vulnerable to attack by a suspect and/or being silhouetted as you make your entry through the doorway or opening. The "fatal funnel" extends from the doorway or opening inward approximately 3' to 4' then outward at a 45° angle to the back outside corners of the room. If you were to picture a funnel on its side in the doorway with the spout of the funnel in the doorway and the mouth

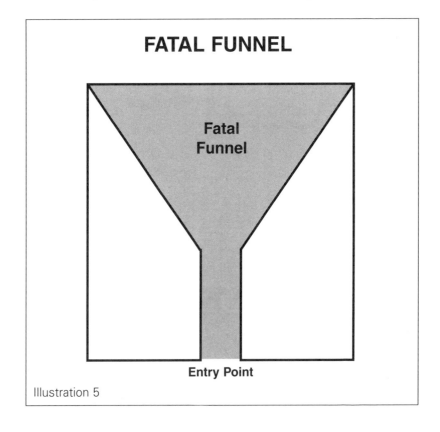

FATAL FUNNEL

Fatal
Funnel

Entry Point

Illustration 5

of the funnel in the room, you will get a better understanding of what is meant by the "fatal funnel."

With this thought in mind, it is important for you to move through this area as quickly as possible. To do this, you must clear the deadly corners first. You can "preliminarily" clear the deadly corners by using a mirror, or using the quick peek method, which I do not recommend because of the unknown factor of the corners. To "absolutely" clear the deadly corners you have to enter the room. Once you have committed yourself to entering the room, the more traditional method of clearing is from the center outward. In other words your attention is directed to the center of the room and not the deadly corners where the threat may be. If you use the alternative methods as described in Alternative Positioning and Entry Tactics below, this sequence is reversed. As you move through the entry point your attention is immediately directed to the corner, then redirected back to the center of the room. Your peripheral vision will pick up any movement that may come from the center of the room as you move through the entry point.

Alternative Entry Positioning and Tactic: Although I have used the traditional entry method described above, I am more comfortable addressing the deadly corner first, then redirecting my attention inward towards the center of the room. Because of this, I modified the way I or my search team would position themselves and enter a room. These modifications are based on the theory that the entry team should be able to see 80 to 90 percent of their area of responsibility of the room before making entry. As you will see, the alternative methods I recommend using will give you a greater tactical advantage of positioning outside the room and when entering the room or area to be searched.

The alternative entry position is accomplished by standing at a slight angle facing inward towards the opening and slightly facing each other. You should be back from the door opening far enough that your weapon or any part of your body can't be seen by the suspects. This position allows you to see the larger open area of the room you are about to enter. Because of your relative position to the door, it permits greater ease of using a mirror, or slicing-the-pie as a clearing technique. Again, because of your relative positioning outside the door, entering the room from that position causes you to automatically direct your attention to the deadly corners.

The time it takes to scan and identify the open area and deadly or hard corner simultaneously is almost imperceptible. Use your peripheral vision to see around you as well as in front of you. If there is any movement, or object to your side, which demands your attention, your peripheral vision should pick it up, thus allowing you to direct your attention to it. This takes practice and training on how to use your peripheral vision to its fullest capabilities. Once the deadly or hard corner has been cleared, your attention is redirected back to your area of responsibility in the larger areas of the room. Do not develop tunnel vision. Dominate your area of responsibility with your weapon. You should be in the combat stance with the weapon held in the Master Grip, see Chapter 7, directing it to address any problem you may encounter while searching the room.

The following explanations of the entry tactics are described using the alternative method I have suggested. This does not alter your basic tactics and areas of responsibilities when entering a room. The following explanations, tactics, and areas of responsibility still apply, even if you choose to use the traditional method of entry; clearing from the center of the room outward.

Executing the Maneuvers: For simplicity, I have used the term "doorway" when referring to the entry point, although an entry point could be any type of opening where the entry team can safely enter the building without having to climb a ladder, or use some other means to enable access through the entry point to conduct their search.

A silent three-count signal is used to execute the entry maneuver. The count can be given by hand, a nod of the head, bobbing the body up and down, or simply silently mouthing the numbers "1," "2," "3." Using a count or hand signal avoids placing the team in jeopardy by having one member move too soon or too late.

To successfully execute any entry tactic, it is easier if you number yourselves, #1 and #2. It makes no difference which number you are, as long as you both understand which number is going to move first. If there are more than two officers on the search team, the succeeding officers are numbered accordingly. When they take up their positions on opposite sides of the entry point, odd numbers are on one side, and even numbers are on the other side. This is done for the sake of simplicity and allows for multiple persons to be on the team without becoming confused as to where they are positioned and what their area of responsibility will be if assigned by number. This method can be altered to fit the entry and search plans. If the team is lined up on the same side of the entry point, they would normally line up in numerical order, 1, 2, 3, 4, etc.

Entry Tactics

Again, the term "doorway" is used when referring to the entry point. As mentioned earlier in this chapter, there are three basic entry methods, which can be used, individually or jointly, by the search team to enter and move through a building in a tactical manner. In order to use these techniques it is important to know and understand their basic principles. The entry tactics described are performed by using the alternative positioning method I have suggested.

Crossing Pattern—X Entry: I believe officers who have not worked or trained with each other will usually find this method to be the easiest to use. It is a simple, no-nonsense tactic to execute, and requires little training to be able to perform it successfully. It permits visual contact between the officers, and eliminates the need to turn your attention from the doorway. It makes it easy to clear the center and corners of the room as you enter because you are already facing inward as you cross through the doorway. This technique also provides stability and maneuverability while carrying your weapon and flashlight.

To execute the crossing pattern, each officer takes a position on opposite sides of the doorway facing each other at a slight angle inward towards the doorway, giving you visual contact with each other as you prepare to make entry. Your weapons are carried in the master grip at the low ready position or low combat stance.

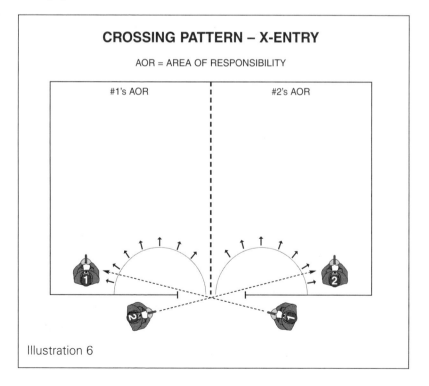

CROSSING PATTERN – X-ENTRY

AOR = AREA OF RESPONSIBILITY

#1's AOR #2's AOR

Illustration 6

When the signal to go is given, one officer goes right and one officer goes left through the doorway. There is a slight delay between the movement of the first and second officer to prevent "jamming up" in the doorway. Once you clear the doorway, rather than use the traditional method of clearing, the position you are now in permits you to naturally clear the deadly or hard corner first, then move outward to the center of the room. Once you have cleared the entry point, each of you takes a position along the wall, 3' to 4' in from the doorway if possible, dominating the room with your weapons, then stop, look, and listen, before proceeding with the search plan. If there are more than two officers on the search team, the other officers should remain outside the room until called in by their teammates.

Photos 6.9 – 6.12 – Crossing Pattern: Outside View

Photos 6.13 – 6.16 – Crossing Pattern: Inside View

Line Entry: When using the line entry all members of the search team enter from the same side of the doorway. The line entry generally requires moving across the doorway opening to the inside far wall of the room. Speed is essential to clear the doorway to allow the second officer immediate access and to avoid silhouetting. This type of entry is used when the search team is unable to use the crossing pattern because of a wall or other restrictions and obstacles.

In preparation for the line entry, the officers take up a position on the right or left side of the doorway, in tandem with each other. Your weapons are carried in the master grip in the low ready position. The lead officer nods his head to signal the entry. The first officer to make entry immediately

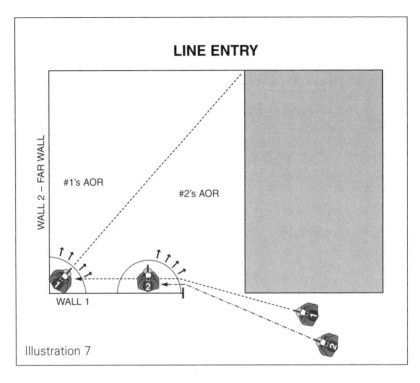

LINE ENTRY

Illustration 7

clears the deadly corner nearest him, moves quickly down the wall to a defensive position and dominates the room with his weapon. The second officer moves instantaneously behind the first officer, clearing the center of the room then the corners nearest him (if applicable) as they enter.

Once the officers clear the doorway they position themselves along the wall, maintaining 5' to 10' distance between them when tactically possible. While dominating the room with their weapons, they stop, look, and listen, then proceed with their search plan. If there are more than two officers on the search team, the other officers should remain outside the room until called in by their teammates.

This entry method is a good example of why I advocate the use of mirrors. By using a mirror to clear the entry point and corners when tactically possible, the risk to the first officer through the door is reduced significantly. This entry method can be executed more safely by using a "limited penetration" tactic that dominates the majority of the room as the team enters. Limited Penetration is discussed later.

Buttonhook—Wrap Around: Normally, the buttonhook or wrap around entry is executed with officers positioned on opposite sides of the entry point, but it can also be done with both of you on the same side of the doorway, such as the position taken in a line entry. The maneuver requires you to "hook and wrap" around the doorjamb nearest to you.

To execute the buttonhook, the officers take a position on opposite sides of the doorway facing each other at a slight angle facing slightly inward toward the doorway. This position is the same position you would assume on the crossing pattern which gives you visual contact with each other as you prepare to make entry, and allows you to see the center area of the room before you enter, eliminating the need to focus fully on the center of the room as you enter. Your weapon is carried in the master grip at the low ready position. Just prior to the actual execution of the entry, you can "hook" the doorjamb with your off hand, or support hand to give you stability and a balance point when you move, or you can simply step (wrap) around the jamb into the room.

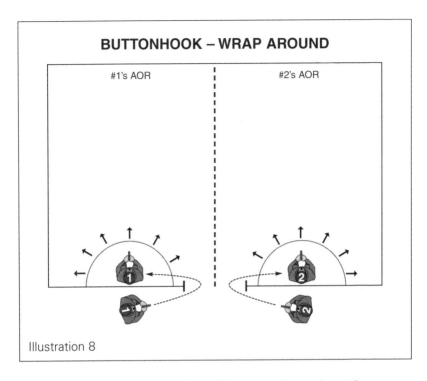

BUTTONHOOK – WRAP AROUND

#1's AOR   #2's AOR

Illustration 8

On the signal to go, the officer on the right side wraps around the doorjamb and into the room to the right of the entry point. The officer on the left side wraps around the doorjamb and into the room to the left of the entry point. There is a slight delay between the movement of the first and second officer to prevent "jamming up" in the doorway. Once the corners are cleared, each of you takes a position along the wall, dominating the room with your weapons, then stop, look, and listen, before proceeding with the search. If there are more than two officers on the search team, the other officers should remain outside the room until called in by their teammates.

One of the primary problems with the buttonhook is the fact that the eyes cannot track as fast as the head and body move, leaving you little choice but to generally see and clear only the center of the room before you can actually see and clear the deadly corner. Your peripheral vision is severely hampered by this movement.

Officer Safety Reminders: As previously discussed, you should always be aware of and know that you may have to enter through windows or other openings that may not allow the use of these entry tactics or the clearing methods previously outlined. For this reason all entry and search plans must be flexible. There are no set, standard clearing methods. For example, you may have to alter your entry and clearing methods. This could be because of a multitude of variances, e.g., limited entry because of obstacles, not enough room for both officers to enter together, unable to position yourself facing inward to the opening causing you to have to turn into the doorway as you go through it, etc. If you have devised new entry and clearing methods that work well and utilize good officer safety practices, then you should share these tactics with your fellow officers. Innovation and imagination are a large part of clearing and entry tactics. This is how the tactics we are discussing in this book were devised and perfected. You should never think you are limited to "standard," "traditional" or "routine" methodology when it comes to your safety and the safety of the citizens you are sworn to protect and serve.

To accomplish the mission successfully, officer safety must not be jeopardized beyond the capabilities of the search team, or to the extent the risk is greater than the result.

Never compromise officer safety for simplicity sake, or to save time and effort.

Movement Tactics

Walls: When talking about moving along walls, there are some who advocate the officer literally "hug" the wall as he moves down a hallway, around a room, or takes a position against a wall while dominating a room. I believe this is a bad technique and seriously violates good officer safety tactics. You should **never hug a wall** or **brush against it** as you move. The proper tactic is to stay 8" to 12" from the wall. There are several reasons for this you may not think about when conducting a building search. Realistically, it is almost impossible to move around a room using a wall because of the obstacles contained in the room. The most likely places you would move down a wall would be hallways and enclosed stairwells. Listed below are some of the most compelling reasons not to hug a wall:

- *Hugging the wall gives you a false sense of security.*

  It makes you believe you have cover because you are against a solid object. Bullets, and certain edged weapons can easily penetrate an inner or outer wall.

- *Today's construction materials make it easy to ricochet a bullet off an inside or outside wall.*

Depending on the angle at which it is fired, a ricochet bullet will travel 4" to 8" from the wall as it traverses down the wall. If an officer is against the wall, then obviously that bullet would strike him.

- *Plaster, dry wall, or similarly constructed walls, transmit sound.*

When the officer brushes against the wall as he moves, he transmits his movement down and through the wall. Surprisingly, if the wall is a connecting wall, this movement can be heard one or two rooms away. Your movements are easily followed from inside the room or hallway the wall separates, thereby giving suspects the advantage.

- *When you move against the wall, either as a part of your room clearing technique or while dominating the room with your weapon, the natural tendency is to use the wall for balance.*

Even though it may be subconscious on your part, this reliance on the wall limits your maneuverability, preventing you from being able to pivot or move about freely in either direction to address a problem area.

Hallways: Hallways are always approached cautiously by the search team. You should stop, look, and listen frequently before exposing yourself to the entrance or junctions of hallways. Use a mirror, or "slice-the-pie" to clear these areas.

One of the safer methods for moving down a hallway is to have the cover officer remain at the entry way, using available cover or concealment, and dominate the hallway with his

Photo 6.17 – Limited Penetration Tactic

weapon (using the Limited Penetration tactic – Photo 6.17) while the search officer moves down the hallway to the next point of entry or location to be searched. This is a cover and movement tactic that permits limited exposure to you as the hallway is being traversed.

When using this tactic, the search officer must move down the opposite side of the hallway his partner is dominating. Move slowly, systematically, and quietly, maintaining a low profile. Once the search officer has reached the desired location, he motions the cover officer forward to the new position. The search officer covers the cover officer's movement.

If the search team chooses to clear the hallway together, they must move in a coordinated effort, slowly, systematically, and quietly. This tactic is sometimes referred to as the stagger or offset method of clearing an area. When tactically possible, they should maintain 5' to 10' between them while moving, and at the same time, presenting a low profile. The cover officer is offset from the search officer, thus allowing for officer separation and clear fields-of-fire. When tactically possible, stay the recommended 8" to 12" off the wall.

You should consider the fact that hallways are present in almost every building you will search. You should plan what movement to use before being confronted with the hallway. All hallways may not be wide enough to permit two officers to enter at the same time, or work together using the stagger or leapfrog method in a safe manner. Because of this possibility, you should have an alternate movement plan if the original plan doesn't fit the situation.

Stairways: Stairways, like hallways, are always approached cautiously by the search team. Again, the search team should stop, look, and listen before exposing themselves to the entrance of a stairway. Use a mirror, or slice-the-pie to clear the stairway access or entrance. When moving up or down stairways, the search team will be confronted with multiple problems.

Some believe moving down a stairway is easier than moving up a stairway. I believe moving up a stairway is easier than moving down a stairway. When moving up a stairway the officer has the advantage of balance, coordination, and a good field-of-vision. When moving down a stairway, the officer loses the advantage of balance, coordination, and a good field-of-vision because the body is at an unusual angle, i.e., trying to bend down to see as you move down the stairwell. When tactically possible, I recommend clearing stairways from the bottom up to enhance your officer safety capabilities.

If the stairway is enclosed all the way to the top or bottom, it is like a hallway and can be traversed by using the hallway domination clearing method. If it is open all the way to the top or bottom, using a mirror or dominating from the entry access point are two options the search team may consider to safely traverse the open space whether going up or down. If the stairway has a landing, or cuts back at a right or left turn at a 90° angle over the primary stairway, there are unique tactical considerations used to clear and traverse the stairway safely. Two of these considerations are to use a mirror attached to the end of your baton, or a mirror that extends. By using these types of mirrors, you reduce the chances of a suspect seeing you as you come up the stairs.

The search team may elect to use the options of the open stairway clearing method, using weapon domination, and mirrors. Or they may choose to traverse together, one moving backwards, facing upwards towards the cut-back area, while the other moves forward, facing the landing to the cut-back as they move simultaneously up the stairs. If this is the chosen method, I strongly recommend the use of a mirror at the landing and cutback areas. Suspects can position themselves on a stair recess above where the search team is approaching and, with relative ease, conceal themselves until it is too late for the search team to effectively react to their presence.

When simultaneously moving up or down the stairs, move in a coordinated effort, slowly, systematically, and quietly. Maintain a distance of 5' to 10' between each other when tactically possible. Present a low profile, with the cover officer offset from the search officer, providing officer separation and clear fields-of-fire. Stay 8" to 12" off the wall. Using the leapfrog method in a stairway can be too congested, creating an officer safety issue of crossfire and jamming the search team together.

I do not recommend officers lie on their backs to clear a stairway. Although this tactic has been advocated, I feel it places the officer at a distinct disadvantage. This is not a natural position from which to move in a tactical manner. When on your back, you have to think about how to push yourself up the stairway while trying to concentrate on what problem area you may be encountering, causing you to lose the edge you need to stay alert to danger, jeopardizing your officer safety tactics, which could result in serious injury or death to an officer if faced with an armed suspect. And, this position makes it extremely difficult to successfully maneuver out of danger if it presents itself.

When formulating the search plan, consider that stairways may be present in the building to be searched. The search team should always discuss a possible stairway clearing method.

Photos 6.18 – 6.23 – Stairway Clearing

6.21

6.22

6.23

Even if a building is single story, a stairway could exist. For example, the building may have an attic access, a basement, or a cellar that is unknown to the search team until entry has been made. Above all else, take your time as you search the stairway, don't hurry yourself and become frustrated because you can't go up or down stairs in a normal manner.

Additional Safety Points: Regardless of which entry and clearing method you use, do not pass open or closed doorways, closets or cupboards without searching and/or securing them first. When doors are located across from each other, or so near each other they prevent the search team from searching and securing them safely, the team must decide which room to enter first. Once the decision is made as to which room to enter first, you should wedge or tie off the opposite door, or doors. This is done in such a manner that a suspect would have to use considerable force to open the door, allowing the search team to hear the disturbance and direct their attention to the threat. Refer to ropes and wedges in Chapter 2.

If the door is to be wedged, force the wedge under the door on the "knob" side of the door. Force the door upward as much as possible so the passage bolt is forced into the strike plate.

To tie off doors, the rope must be pulled tight; the door is tied off in such a manner that the doors have a counter movement against each other.

Photo 6.24 – Limited Penetration

Weapon Domination Tactics

Limited Penetration: This is a tactical maneuver used from a position of cover or concealment, such as a wall or similar type of barricade. It is used primarily to dominate a room, a specific danger area, a large open area, hallway, or stairwell with your weapon while one or more members of the search team enter, search and clear the dominated area.

To avoid silhouetting, or at least minimize it, and to present as small a target as possible, approximately 95 to 98 percent of your body is behind the medium being used as cover or concealment. The only part of your body that should be exposed is slightly less than half your head and that part of your arm and weapon hand that you extend into the area you want to dominate. To execute the maneuver, lean into the medium being used, which will give you better balance and maneuverability, and extend your weapon into the room and dominate the room with its presence, holding the weapon in a single-hand master grip.

Once the cover officer is in position, the search team enters the room. As they enter, they must be conscious of the cover officer's weapon by maintaining a low profile so as not to interfere with his fields-of-vision and fields-of-fire. When the team makes its initial entry, the cover officer is dominating the entire room by scanning back and forth with his weapon. As the team begins its search, the cover officer redirects his weapon to cover the areas away from where the search team is searching. The search team moves systematically to search and control the room. They control any suspects found in the room. The cover officer does not leave his position if this occurs. It is important for the cover officer to keep his attention on the areas he is covering with his weapon. In other words, wherever he looks, so too does the weapon.

As with any entry technique or tactic, clearing as much of the room or area as you can before entering, or executing any domination technique, is always the wisest thing to do. This tactic, when applied under the right circumstance, provides an added measure of safety to the search team because the covering officer's sole responsibilities are to insure all danger areas are covered that the search team can't while conducting their search.

Caution! Because of the presence of the weapon in the room as officers are entering, there are built in officer safety concerns when applying the Limited Penetration technique.

- The immediate presence of cross-fire situations, and
- Moving into the covering officer's fields-of-vision and fields-of-fire.

Because of the inherent dangers involved with using this tactic, it is my strong recommendation that you not use it until you have had training in its proper use.

CHAPTER 7
SEARCH TACTICS

Communication

Effective communication is of the utmost importance for the successful operation of any tactical situation. Communication not only refers to radio traffic, but also to the manner and means by which the search team communicates with each other, whether verbally or silently. Radio traffic should be kept to an absolute minimum. It is important to maintain radio discipline between members of the search team, and between the search team and perimeter team. Unnecessary dialogue heightens the chances of creating confusion between the search team and perimeter team. Violating radio discipline could also compromise the safety of the search team. The more the search team has to talk, the easier it is for suspects to hear them and plot their movement through the building.

When transmitting on the radio, use low audio communication tactics. You should place your mouth as close to the microphone as possible and speak softly, slowly, and clearly, so you are understood by your partner and the perimeter team, but not the suspect. Refer to the discussion of portable radios in Chapter 1.

You should be able to communicate between yourselves through hand signals and/or eye contact when possible. It is important to discuss and practice what a head gesture might mean, or the movement of the eyes, etc., before being used in a critical situation when the radio can't be used safely. Silent communication can also be accomplished by the use of sign language. There are several "survival signing" courses on the market for law enforcement. This type of communication is being used more and more by tactical teams. By learning the basic alphabet and applying it to law enforcement use, signing can become a valuable tool at any given time when a silent command or gesture is needed to communicate some warning of danger, or to have a partner move to a more tactical advantage, such as a pedestrian contact or vehicle stop.

There are numerous SWAT publications, which contain illustrations of commonly used hand signals. In most instances, the number of hand signals can range from 15 or 20 and upwards to 45 or 50. However, you don't need to use that many, and quite frankly very few SWAT teams use that many. I suggest you get the book entitled, *SWAT TEAM Development and Deployment,* by Michael Holm, a retired DEA operator, published by Varro Press, Shawnee Mission, Kansas. The author illustrates numerous hand signals used by SWAT teams, from the basic to advanced. I would recommend you getting agent Holm's book and select 10 or so hand signals for use by your patrol force, ensure everyone knows them and put them in use any time silent communications are needed, be it a building search or vehicle stop, they can be a life saving tool in tense situations where your safety is put in jeopardy if verbal communications aren't possible or appropriate to use.

The Search Triangle

This is a simple and effective tactical maneuver using the triangulation theory of conducting a search. The imaginary top point of the triangle is directed to a perceived problem area, the area to be searched, or where a suspect is likely to be. The bottom right and left points of the triangle are the search and cover officers. It doesn't matter which corner the search and cover officers occupy.

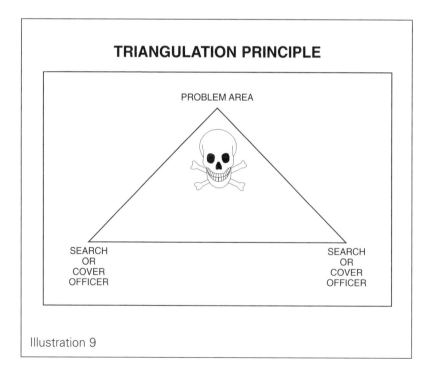

TRIANGULATION PRINCIPLE

PROBLEM AREA

SEARCH OR COVER OFFICER

SEARCH OR COVER OFFICER

Illustration 9

This maneuver provides added officer safety for the search team. It allows for clear fields-of-fire as you move through a room and it permits visual contact between the cover and search officer.

The formation is flexible, rotating, and changing as the room configuration or situation changes. Maintaining a true triangle configuration is not tactically possible. However, maintaining its basic configuration principle is, and I recommend this tactic be used as often as possible to maintain the level of safety it provides.

Triangulation is used during suspect contacts inside the building, when tactically possible. Triangulation can also be

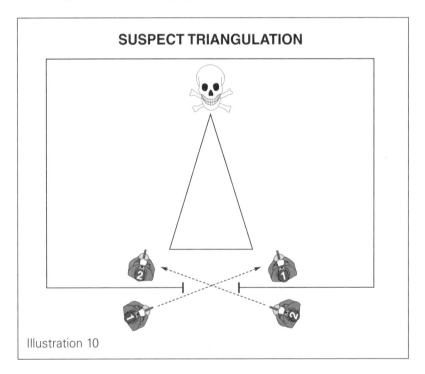

SUSPECT TRIANGULATION

Illustration 10

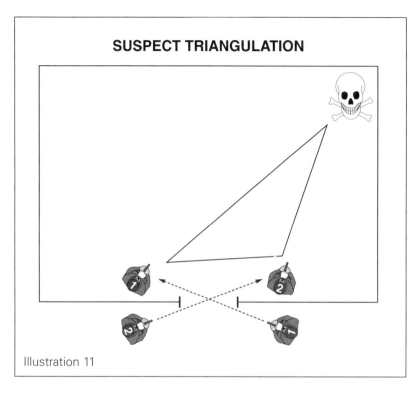

Illustration 11

used in other suspect contacts you will be involved in as a part of your duties, such as pedestrian approaches or removing suspects from a vehicle, etc.

The purpose of triangulation is to divide the suspect's attention between two or more officers, thus giving the officers the tactical advantage.

Carrying The Weapon

When making entry into the building and while conducting the search, your weapon is drawn and carried in the *Master Grip*. All weapons are carried in the double-action battery.

Photos 7.1 – 7.2 – The Master Grip

The Master Grip: It is imperative you learn how to carry your weapon in the master grip. The concept of the master grip is a natural position and is an extension of eye-hand coordination. The finger points down the long axis of the weapon at the top of the trigger well. When you point the weapon at a potential danger area, it is naturally pointed to where your attention is directed. When you assume target acquisition, the front site of the weapon is almost automatically aligned with the center portion of whatever you have pointed the weapon at. When a threat presents itself, the finger is moved down to engage the trigger. Target identification and acquisition, coupled with site alignment when required, lend themselves naturally to the master grip. This safety feature is not to be confused with "point shooting" techniques.

The FBI and the US military conducted tests which have shown the master grip concept does not deter the ability of an individual to quickly and accurately engage a threat and

Photos 7.3 – 7.4 – Low Ready Position

neutralize it. Furthermore, over the past 20-plus years, there has not been a single SWAT-team I have had contact with that does not endorse the master grip concept for team and individual officer safety.

Low Ready Position: The weapon is normally carried using two-hands with the master grip, and is carried at or just below eye level, ergo, the low ready position. This tactic is considered to be a modified Weaver stance, with the off hand, or support hand, supporting the strong hand. The weapon is extended forward and at a slight downward angle, as you are moving through the building. To garner the full effect of the weapon's dominance, you must look over the top of the weapon as you search and move. The position of the weapon is why some refer to this as the "low ready" position. This method permits fairly rapid target acquisition by moving the weapon slightly up or down when confronted with a suspect or potential threat. The low ready, as demonstrated, could be exhausting. The positioning of the weapon, extended outward from the chest, along with the weapon's weight, requires you to use the shoulder, neck, and arm muscles to carry it. Carrying the weapon in this manner also makes it difficult to move tactically through a building without exposing the weapon as you round a corner or enter a room.

In recent years, this method has been modified considerably, almost to the identical method I developed in the mid 1980's, as the Modified Combat Stance and Hold.

In the Modified Combat Stance and Hold, the weapon is held close to the midsection in the area of the solar plexus and parallel to the ground, reducing the stress to the muscles of the neck, shoulders and arms.

The Modified Combat Stance and Hold: The weapon is carried in the master grip, arms slightly bent with the elbows held close to your sides, while holding the weapon close to the body in line with the solar plexus. Carrying the weapon in the modified combat stance with a two-hand hold takes less strength and endurance to hold it in a ready position for extended periods of time. Because the arms are flexed slightly inward, the weight of the weapon is distributed between

Photo 7.5 – The Modified Combat Stance and Hold

the arms and shoulders. The reason I call this position a modified combat stance is because you are already in position to address any threat that may present itself, without having to modify your basic body position or eye contact.

In this position, the weapon is generally pointed at what would be the suspect's mid-section and pelvic area, or the

Photo 7.6 – The Modified Combat Stance and Hold

general lower portion of center body mass. If a threat is encountered, moving the weapon upward to center body mass—the chest area—is a natural movement. Your lower peripheral vision will pick up the weapon moving upward to the point that the weapon and threat are in the same sight alignment and you have not lost any tactical positioning or are required to exert any extra movement to address the threat. Another advantage to this tactic is that by simply removing your off hand, or support hand, you can easily control the weapon with your strong hand, thus allowing you to use your off hand to open doors, move something, hold a flashlight, retain your OC, etc. I have found this takes less concentration on where the weapon is, as it is automatically pointing where I am looking, and it is a more natural position from which I can look over the weapon to conduct the search.

The modified combat stance, with either the two-hand hold or single-hand hold gives you better control of the weapon, and is easier to move with because the weapon is not extended outward with locked elbows. Keeping the weapon closer to the body provides for better weapon retention, which lessens the chance of someone grabbing it as you move through an opening, around a corner, look over an obstacle, etc.

When the weapon is carried and handled properly in the modified combat stance, such as crossing in front of each other, preparing to make entry into another room, moving rapidly across open areas, etc., it is easily lowered and raised when necessary for officer safety, while maintaining complete control of the weapon and your area of responsibility.

Lowering the weapon often results in the officer actually pointing the weapon at the ground, or at an angle away from his partner to avoid a crossfire situation, thereby diverting your visual attention, which leaves your area of responsibility totally uncovered or dominated by the weapon. When you lower your weapon for any reason, do not lower it more than a 30 to 40° angle to the ground, and lower it directly in front of you or in-line with the threat area you are covering with the weapon. By doing this you offer a less dangerous crossfire situation while you keep your eyes on the problem area, and maintain a tactically advantageous position with your weapon. As stated earlier, we will never be able to completely avoid crossfire situations, however we can reduce them to less threatening situations.

Modified Combat Stance with Single Hand Hold: When the situation demands, the weapon can be held in a modified combat stance with a single-hand hold. An example would be in close quarters, such as hallways, moving up stairways, going through doorways, opening closets or doors, looking over an obstacle, or holding a flashlight away from your weapon.

The weapon is held at waist level, 4" to 6" in front of and just above the hip. As with the two-hand hold, the weapon is generally pointed at what would be the suspect's mid-section and pelvic area, or the general lower portion of center body mass. If a threat is encountered, moving the weapon upward to center body mass – the chest area – is a natural movement. Caution should be taken when carrying the weapon in this position. If held too close to the body, you could cause the weapon to malfunction and jam if clothing or other objects get caught in the cylinder or slide when it is fired, and you could suffer powder burns.

Transitioning strong-hand to off-hand: Finally, the modified combat stance allows you to quickly and easily transition from your strong hand to your off hand, or support hand, without taking time to look at your weapon and lose sight of your area of responsibility.

Where the eyes look, the weapon looks. The weapon precedes your movements. Wherever you look, or direct your attention, the weapon is pointed at your center of attention, e.g., a suspect, a danger area such as a closed door or a possible hiding place, etc. By carrying the weapon in a tactical manner, it leads you into a room, around a corner, up stairs, down a hallway, behind a chair or couch, etc.

In Photos 7.7 and 7.8, the weapon is transitioned to the single-hand hold without losing target acquisition or changing your balance or body position to perform other tasks with your off hand. These tasks could be directing the

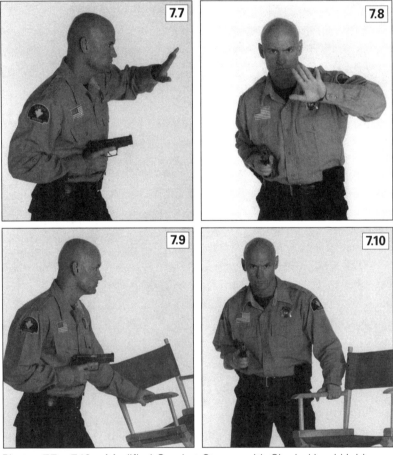

Photos 7.7 – 7.10 – Modified Combat Stance with Single Hand Hold

suspect to move or deflecting an object that may be thrown by the suspect.

In Photos 7.9 and 7.10, the weapon is transitioned to the single-hand hold, while the off hand is used to move an object. Again this is accomplished without affecting your body position or losing weapon domination of the area being searched.

Silhouetting

Silhouetting creates a negative factor for the successful completion of any mission. The officer's inability to move safely without being compromised by light is critical to the success or failure of their mission.

It is my firm belief most officers don't understand what silhouetting really is. This phenomenon occurs during daylight and darkness. It happens on car stops, at domestic violence calls, and while searching buildings. Avoiding this situation is a basic officer safety issue that has been pounded into the heads of all of us from day one of the basic academy, yet rookies and veteran officers alike continue to silhouette themselves or their partners.

The easiest way to explain how to avoid silhouetting is to simply state; any time there is light behind you, above you, or beside you, you can be silhouetted. A flashlight beam crossing in front of you or behind you, whether you are moving or standing still, can silhouette you, even if you're the one carrying the flashlight, or it can silhouette your partner.

Light Sources: Patrol unit lights, alley lights, spot lights, flashlights, street lights, house lights, emergency lights, etc., are just some of the light sources which can silhouette you when you are trying to move in a tactical manner, whether crossing in front of the light source, standing to the side of it, or remaining near the outer edges of the "halo-of-light" emitted from the source. The "halo-of-light" is that extreme edge of the pattern of light where form and shadow are distinguishable.

Ambient Light: The presence of ambient light is something most of us don't understand or think about when we are involved in an incident. Ambient light can be natural or man made. It is a light source capable of allowing one to distinguish forms and shadows. Generally, this type of light comes from the moon, a street light, or other light sources in the area surrounding the location of the officer. The light source is normally behind, or at an oblique angle to your position. To avoid being silhouetted by ambient light, you must always be aware of the lighting conditions present at the scene, and know what light sources produce ambient light.

Other Sources: There are ways of being silhouetted other than by a direct source of light. Standing in front of open doors or windows. Walking along a roofline or ridge-line, moving without using cover or concealment. If you can imagine seeing your form or shadow, then you are probably a silhouette.

To recognize the possibility of being silhouetted, either by direct or ambient light, you must take the time to stop and look around your immediate position before moving or committing yourself, then move in a tactical manner to reduce or eliminate being silhouetted. You should also be aware that your unit lights can create an ambient light effect, or a direct silhouette effect, when the parking lights, flashers, turn signals, overhead lights, etc., are on.

Using The Flashlight

There has been much discussion about the use of lights and lighting systems by officers. Most of the discussion concerns the pros and cons of what brand of flashlight to use, how powerful it should be and how the officer should use the light in a tactical manner. In this chapter, I want to address the tactical use of the flashlight, as well as brightness and type. For you to be tactical, whether in a building search or just needing the light to see, you should first consider why you are using the flashlight.

When using the flashlight to illuminate an area it should be done with three objectives in mind.

1. Illuminate the area so you can see what is inside.

2. Blind and disorient a suspect who may be hiding in that area.

3. Protect you from being seen by a suspect because your light is too intense for him to see through.

One of the more difficult techniques to master is the use of the flashlight in coordination with the weapon. Since most patrol officers don't have the convenience of a "tac-light" attached to their duty weapon, they need to understand how to properly use the flashlight and duty weapon together. To effectively and efficiently master this technique, training is important. It is not just being able to carry the weapon and the flashlight together, it is the ability to use them in perfect coordination with each other; letting one enhance the other without conscious thought.

For you to effectively use your flashlight in a tactical manner, I will discuss how to use it by using what I call a "burst of light," and why I believe this is a good tactic. I will also discuss how to carry the flashlight with the weapon and what oblique lighting is and how it can be used.

Burst-of-Light: Whether moving into a room, looking into a confined area, or trying to identify an object or form, it is best to use the flashlight in a controlled light discipline. This is the "burst-of-light" technique. It is a one or two-second "burst of light" directed into the area you want to see, or at a suspect you want to illuminate.

With your attention directed to a specific area, object, or form you want to identify, all you need do is push the button and project a "burst of light" into or at the location to be illuminated. This lights the area long enough for you to identify what you see. This tactic can greatly reduce, if not eliminate, the accidental silhouetting of you and other members of the search team. It also reduces the negative effect the light has on your night vision when in a darkened environment.

If you illuminate a suspect with a "burst of light" it will cause him a temporary loss of vision. This will allow you to tactically move from your original location to a position of advantage before reestablishing contact or communication with the suspect. This is accomplished by moving quickly to your right or left. Reestablish contact with the suspect from your new position by shining the light directly into his eyes to mask you and your partner's position and movement. Take verbal control of the suspect and place them at a position of disadvantage to be searched and handcuffed.

The Crossover Method: One of the easiest methods of carrying the flashlight and weapon together is the crossover support method. The crossover method is effective with most flashlights and is normally used with a large flashlight, such as a three to five cell, so long as the light is activated by a "push" of the finger. To form the crossover platform, the weapon is carried in the master grip. The wrist areas of the strong and off hand, or support hand are crossed over each other, thus the reference to "crossover." The flashlight hand becomes a platform for the weapon hand. The bottom portion of the weapon hand wrist rests on top of the flashlight hand wrist. Pressure against the top and bottom wrist is subtly applied for stability. You must take care not to cause muscle stress and fatigue by pushing too hard with either hand.

Photos 7.11 – 7.12 – The Crossover Method with a large flashlight

The flashlight is held palm down in the off hand, or support hand. The push button is controlled by the index finger, middle finger, thumb, or palm of the hand, depending on the type of flashlight being used. When the need to turn on the light presents itself, you simply push the button when you have directed the light and weapon to the area you wish to illuminate. This method is extremely effective with the tac-light. You hold the tac light in the same manner that you do a large flashlight when employing the Crossover Method.

Modified Flashlight Hold: This technique utilizes a tac-light with an end cap push button switch. The heel of the hand is used to turn the flashlight on and off. The flashlight used in Photos 7.15 and 7.16, is the SureFire 6Z Combat Light®. It has a grommet on the tube that helps you secure the flashlight when using it in tandem with your weapon regardless of what hold you use or how you grip it, and it

Photos 7.13 – 7.14 – The Crossover Method with smaller tactical light

has a push button on the back of the tube for tactical applications. I recommend employing the tac-light in what I call a "modified flashlight hold." This is done by placing the flashlight between the ring finger and forefinger of the support hand. Place the rear of the light so the push button is securely against the fatty part of the heel of the hand. The light is gripped by applying slight pressure with the fingers

Photos 7.15 – 7.16 – Modified Flashlight Hold with SureFire 6Z Combat Light®

and palm. Carrying the flashlight in this manner only requires a slight amount of pressure to turn on the light by squeezing the fingers as though you were going to make a fist, which forces the push button into the heel of the hand. Conversely, releasing the pressure, or opening the hand slightly, turns off the light. Carrying the light to the side of the weapon, instead of the crossover method, allows you to move the weapon and light together, or move the light away from the weapon when the need arises, without altering the single hand hold of the low-ready position or the modified combat stance and hold.

As with any technique or tactic, you should train with it before using it in a tactical situation. The more proficient you become at coordinating your weapon and flashlight together, the less you will have to think about it. This will allow you to concentrate on searching the building.

Those flashlights which can only be turned on and off by "twisting" the tube or head present a unique tactical problem, whether or not they are being used in the crossover method. You must become extremely proficient with this type of flashlight to operate it with one hand. This type of light also limits your ability to effectively deliver bursts-of-light because of the extended time it takes to turn the flashlight on and off. My personal recommendation is to not use these types of flashlights in tactical situations.

Oblique Lighting Technique: Another tactical use of the flashlight is to use it obliquely. This is a relatively simple form of illumination that may require prolonged use of the flashlight to illuminate a room or area. This is accomplished by turning on the flashlight, laying it on the floor or ground, and pointing it into the room or area to be illuminated. You then simply squat or kneel down to look over the halo-of-light to identify shapes or forms. When using this form of lighting, you must remember to remain behind cover or concealment, ensuring you are not silhouetted by the halo-of-light created by the flashlight. If the light is placed inside the entry point, it must be turned off or picked up before making entry.

Oblique Lighting Technique with a Mirror: If there is a portion of a room or area into which you cannot readily see, you can illuminate it by using a mirror and a flashlight. The flashlight beam is directed at an oblique angle onto the mirror. By directing the mirror into the area to be illuminated you will be able to identify shape and form.

This is a limited use tactic, requiring three officers to safely perform it. One officer handles the mirror and flashlight, the second officer uses another mirror, or looks into the area where the light is being directed, and the third officer covers the other two. Again, when using this tactic, you must remember to remain behind cover or concealment, ensuring you are not silhouetted by the halo-of-light created by the flashlight, or the light coming from the mirror. And, as always, you should practice and train using this tactic before trying to apply it in a real situation.

This technique should only be used when there are no other means available to light an area, and it should never be used if only two officers are present.

Night Vision

We should all be aware of what night vision is and how it alters our ability to see in low light conditions, be it night or day. When we go from one light source to another our vision is impaired, from slight impairment to being almost blind, because our eyes are not capable of adjusting rapidly to the change. Because of this, it is foolish to believe you will be able to maintain controlled lighting conditions which will allow your night vision to be totally effective. It is just as foolish for you to believe you will be able to see in the dark as well as you can in the light.

Searching a building at night exposes you to a variety of lighting conditions, and because of this, your eyes never fully adjust or adapt to any given light condition. Without going into all the medical terminology and explanations, it is sufficient to say that the human eye is not capable of true night vision, therefore we must learn to develop and protect our limited night vision capability.

Developing Night Vision: How does one develop night vision? It begins with a proper diet. Vitamin A is an important part of that diet, however, you don't have to go out and gobble up Vitamin A pills. As long as you maintain a well balanced diet, you will get all the Vitamin A you need. If you believe additional Vitamin A is needed, seek the advice of your doctor before supplementing your diet just because you think you need to enhance your vision.

To help your eyes become acclimated to darkness you need to learn to rely less on lights and more on your own sight capabilities. This principle is one that goes hand-in-hand with my theory of "bursts-of-light" when using your flashlight. It requires self discipline on your part to resist the desire to walk with your flashlight turned on, flashing it around "just to see what's there," or to turn on lights when there is enough light with which to see.

There are a couple of axioms regarding lights and vision.

1. When going from light into dark, light it up.

2. When going from dark into light, darken it.

These "rules" are not to be taken as gospel when making a decision to turn lights on or off, but rather, your decision should be based solely on the tactical situation in which you are involved. A few of the most obvious things you need to consider before turning lights on or off are:

1. What are the lighting conditions where the suspect is located?

   a. Is it to your advantage to reverse those conditions?

2. What are the lighting conditions you are in?

3. What are the lighting conditions you will be moving to?

   a. Again, is it to your advantage to alter those conditions?

4. Persons in darkness or shadow can see persons in light.

   a. Conversely, persons in light can't always see persons in darkness or shadow.

5. *If 4 and 4a are correct, why are you standing in the light?*

So, when making the decision about what light conditions you are going to incorporate, always remember that this decision is paramount to your safety.

Aiding your Night Vision: A simple method to aid in the development of your night vision is to close your strong eye while preparing to enter a darkened area from a lighted area, if the situation allows. The longer the eye remains closed, the better chance it has of adjusting to darkness, and the more quickly it will adapt to the darkness when opened. The eye should remain closed two to five minutes or longer if possible. By allowing the strong eye to adjust to darkness it will be easier for you to distinguish shape and form once you have entered a dark area. On average, it takes the eyes up to 30 minutes, and sometimes longer, to fully adjust from one light source to another.

Using night vision equipment: If you have the ability to use night vision goggles or a night vision scope, this is a great advantage and will enhance your ability to move more effectively without using the flashlight. However there are four points to remember when using night vision equipment.

1. Peripheral vision and depth perception are lost.

2. Depending on what generation night vision equipment you use, a sudden bright light will "wash out" the optics and, in effect, "blind" you.

3. Depending on what generation night vision equipment you use, some type of ambient light may be needed for the equipment to function properly. Using a red lens on your flashlight may provide the ambient light necessary but the actual night vision device may be blurred or darkened considerably. Also, by using the red lens, you may create a silhouette effect as well as giving away your position to the suspect.

4. The extended use of night vision dramatically reduces your ability to see effectively once you quit using it. It takes a substantial period of time for your eyes to readjust to normal sight.

I do not recommend using any form of night vision for a building search over extended periods of time, unless there is no other alternative. If one officer is using night vision goggles, the other officer should use a night vision scope. Using the scope will preserve the vision in one eye to the light conditions present. Use the scope with the non-dominant eye. With this method, one officer has the ability to see form and shadow without the night vision equipment if need be.

The disadvantage of the scope is the officer's hands are occupied with the scope, preventing carrying his weapon effectively. If you leave the scope turned on when you remove it from your eye, the glow from the scope, at the least may silhouette you, and at the worst, give away your position.

Use night vision like you would a burst of light; use it in short amounts of time, say 10 to 20 seconds at a time. This seems like a very short time frame, but once you practice with night vision, you will see how effective you can be with it.

Mirroring

When I talk of mirroring by a patrol officer, I am referring to the tactical use of a hand-held mirror, not the tactical mirrors used by SWAT-teams. As mentioned in Chapter 2, the size of the mirror is important. The correct size ensures safe use, and ease of securing it should you need it again.

Like weapons, the use of mirrors often raises debate. Some people say mirrors are unreliable and difficult for a patrol officer to use in tactical situations. Others will say mirrors are the next best thing to magic.

I don't believe mirrors are magic, but I do believe they are an excellent tactical tool the patrol officer should learn to use. It is my opinion that if you can use a mirror to look into, around, above, or under an area, thereby eliminating the need to stick your head into the unknown area, then why not use it? If a suspect decides to attack an officer who is clearing an entry point or other area, it's better to have a broken piece of glass or sore hand, than a broken head or gouged out eye. When used properly, a mirror can be one of your best allies. When used improperly, it can be a major hazard to your safety.

You should use a mirror anytime you feel there is a threat to your safety, when going into an unfamiliar area, or whenever it's tactically possible. A mirror should be used before entering a room, going around a corner, moving into a hallway, going up or down a stairway, looking into a closet, looking into an attic access, looking under a bed, behind a chair, etc., etc., etc. To use a mirror successfully it must be done cautiously and with adequate light so you can see into the area being mirrored. Depending on the type of mirror being used, distance perception can be distorted; objects may appear farther away or closer than they actually are. Also, shapes and shadows can be deceiving.

Holding The Mirror: To use the mirror safely and effectively requires you know how to hold it, at what angles it should be directed, and the proper distances it should be extended.

If you are not using an extension mirror, the mirror should be held along the edges with the *thumb and forefinger,* with either the strong or off hand, depending on which side of the opening you are. If you grasp it between the thumb and forefinger, in a pinching manner, you loose some control and mobility of the mirror. However, there may be instances when this is the only way you can hold the mirror.

To see effectively with the mirror, it should be tilted at a 30 to 45° angle, which will enable you to see into the room directly in front of the doorway, window, or opening being mirrored. Also, by being conscious of the angle at which the mirror

Photo 7.17 – Holding the Mirror

is held, you will avoid displaying your own image or your partner's image to a suspect, by canting it too far up or back.

Using The Mirror: The proper method of using a mirror is to look from the center of the search area outward to the corners. To do this requires holding the mirror near the edge of the doorway, window, or opening, without exposing it unnecessarily. It should be moved slowly and deliberately in a semi-circle pattern at a height and level which affords you the best opportunity to see obstacles or a suspect. If possible, once you have cleared from the center of the room to the corners, move the mirror slowly up and down from the floor to the ceiling to see the entire area you are preparing to enter. Once you are satisfied the area is clear, slowly project

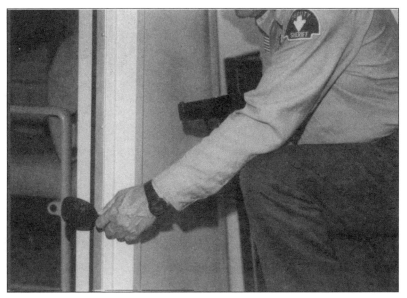

Photo 7.18 – Holding the Mirror

the mirror into the room just beyond the edge of the door-jamb, window, or opening, to check more closely into the deadly or hard corners. Even though you have cleared an entry point with the mirror, this does not eliminate the need for the search team to visually clear the deadly or hard corners of the room as they enter the room.

Caution should be taken not to extend the mirror too far beyond the inner edge of the doorway or opening by exposing your hand or your arm, this should also be remembered when looking under an object or over an object.

Windows, or similar openings, are more difficult to mirror than a doorway. They present unique clearing and entry problems to the search team. Mirror from the corners of the window or opening, clearing the area directly below the corners of the window or opening first. Then, clear inward towards the center of the window or opening, checking directly below the area into which the team will be climbing. Finally, clear outward to the outside corners of the room, or as far into the room as possible.

These tactics and methods are done for two reasons. First, of course, is the obvious, to detect hidden suspects and, second, to locate obstacles which may hinder or prevent the search team from making a safe and successful stealth entry.

The most often used, and in some instances the strongest argument against using mirrors, is they are too time consuming. This argument is often true because the patrol officer doesn't know how to properly use a mirror. If you intend to use a mirror, then, like any other tactical procedure, you must train with it before being confronted with a situation where you need it.

Let me say this about the mirror being "too time consuming," and officer safety. *"It is better to go slow and take your time than it is to go fast and jeopardize your safety."*

CHAPTER 8
SEARCH CONSIDERATIONS AND SUSPECT CONTACT

To effectively search for anything, be it evidence or a person, a systematic, orderly search plan must be adhered to. Gather as much information as you can before you search. Don't let the excitement of the moment create unnecessary risks and hazards. Maintain team integrity and consistency by searching each room or area in the same manner or pattern when tactically possible. The search team will avoid confusion and/or chaotic situations by complimenting and counter-balancing each other. This is accomplished with a proper tactical plan, a systematic search, and constant communication with each other, verbally and visually. It also requires slowing each other down when necessary and reversing or switching rolls as the situation dictates.

Approach Considerations: The primary target must be approached safely prior to conducting the perimeter search. There are patterns around most buildings that will assist you to identify occupancy and avenues of approach. Sidewalks, whether residential or commercial, generally lead to entry and exit doors. Fences and gates are normally in very close proximity to these doors. Traffic patterns on lawns or dirt areas indicate approaches to entry and exit doors when sidewalks are absent. Narrow paths around fence lines or to and from gates may indicate the presence of animals, such as dogs, these paths generally lead from where the animal may sleep or have access to the yard area. Toys in a yard indicate the presence of children. These simple indicators can aid you in making your approaches more safely, and will also aid you in making your entry plans.

Immediate Perimeter Search: Before entry is made, the immediate area around the primary objective must be searched and contained to allow for the safe setting of the inner and outer perimeters. This search is accomplished with the same considerations as the search of a building, by having a good tactical plan for a systematic search of the area. The search can be done in quadrants, linear or circular, depending on the type of area; such as commercial versus residential, types of buildings; e.g., single story, multiple story, stairwells, alcoves, doorways, etc.; type of vegetation, e.g., shrubs, bushes, trees, etc.; vehicles present, lighting or lack of lighting, etc. Be sure to check high ground and all areas of concealment, including vehicles.

Use the helicopter to check rooftops, roadways, fields, etc., and the perimeter for unusual activity you may not detect from ground level. Having the helicopter assist you in the perimeter search also allows you to set up your inner and outer perimeters more effectively. Once they are done, have them leave the area.

Pre-search Options

Once the inner perimeter is set, there are options to be considered before entering the building. Understanding certain human behavioral patterns can make your job a lot easier and safer. It is a natural survival instinct for trapped animals to fight for their freedom or resist capture. This survival instinct is present in humans as well. Given the opportunity to "save face" so to speak, most persons will submit to an officer's authority when confronted with a no-win situation, i.e. suspect caught during the commission of a crime and complying with the demand for surrender.

However, before demanding the suspect's surrender, the inner perimeter must be set. Perimeter officers should be behind cover or concealment. When the demand for surrender is given, the entry team acts as the arrest team by taking a position near the exit where suspects will be directed to come out of the building. The entry/arrest team remains behind cover or concealment until the suspects exit the building. As the suspects exit the building they are given individual verbal commands directing them to a position of advantage for the entry/arrest team to take them into custody. This tactic is not magical it is simply combining good officer safety practices with sound tactical techniques.

To apply the demand for surrender option, there are six basic steps.

1. Set an inner perimeter with an entry/arrest team in place to control the suspects when they leave the building.

2. The officers' presence is announced and surrender of the suspects is demanded.

3. State the conditions of the surrender and the negative consequences if the suspects fail to comply with the demands.

4. A short time limit is set for the suspects to comply when the demand for surrender is given. The actual time limit will be determined by you.

5. The threat of a canine to force compliance should be used. Whether a canine is present or not is irrelevant.

6. Give clear and precise commands as to where the suspects are to exit the building.

Compliance by the suspects with this option does not eliminate the need to search the building. However, it can greatly reduce the hazard of the search when suspects do comply with the surrender demands. The contention that announcing the presence of the officers places them in greater jeopardy is not valid. As stated earlier, the suspects already know you are there and that there is little chance for escape. They also know that eventually you are going to enter the building to apprehend them, so why not present the opportunity for surrender, affording minimal risk to you and the suspects while, at the same time, you clear the building of one or more threats before entering.

Applying Planning Considerations: As the search team enters the building each must know their pre-determined responsibilities, i.e., who will search and who will cover. The two **independent** roles are important factors in conducting a safe building search. Each officer must have faith in the other's ability. The cover officer must cover, and the search officer must search to avoid compromising officer safety. Of course, as with all well made plans, Murphy's Law always applies in these operations. That's why an alternate entry and search plan should be decided on before entering the building. This plan is initiated without delay when necessary. The alternate plan is conceived by asking each other numerous "What if?" questions. By thinking like the suspects you may be able to pre-determine hiding locations and escape routes and effectively take away the suspect's perceived advantages.

To reinforce a prior statement, the search team should use the same tactics throughout the building as much as possible. Their entry and clearing methods when going from room to room should be as consistent as possible to avoid confusion and loss of search integrity. To maintain this concept, the search team must remember to use proper movement tactics, cover, and concealment while inside the building. *And, even though most items inside a building do not afford proper cover, they can provide concealment, and should be used by the search team when possible.* Often times officers become so engrossed with the

Building Search

search they fail to recognize when they are no longer practicing proper officer safety tactics as they conduct the search.

Search Integrity: By conducting a slow, systematic, and deliberate search, the proper officer safety tactics are more likely to be used and the chances of finding the suspects increase significantly, while the chances of an officer being injured or killed is significantly reduced.

Looking for the Suspects

One of the aspects of conducting a thorough search is knowing how to identify what we are looking for. In this instance, we are looking for a suspect, not items of evidence. When we think of looking for someone, quite often the thought comes to mind that we are looking for the whole person. When we search a building, we generally operate on this principle, when in fact, we should be looking for parts of the person, such as concentrating on locating a foot, an elbow, a knee, a hand, a shoulder, etc. These are the parts of the body that usually protrude from under a bed, behind a chair, on a shelf in a closet, behind a door, etc.

You should also look for items of clothing that may not be a part of the environment in which they are located. When a suspect is in a hurry to hide, sometimes a piece of his clothing will be caught in a crack, or protrude from some other area in which they are hiding. By being able to identify an out-of-place piece of clothing, the tip of a shoe, or an elbow, you will be able to determine what tactic to use to clear the area and apprehend the suspect before the suspect is aware of your presence.

Another trick of the trade is to learn how not to look at something you are looking at. This is a technique where you look at an object without looking directly at it. Some refer to it as off-center vision, or simply put, looking at an object at an oblique angle. By focusing attention above, below, to the right, or left of an object, you are able to distinguish forms and images. This is an extremely beneficial technique in low light conditions. It allows you to see better at night, in a semi-darkened room or building, and helps to preserve your night vision without having to use a flashlight.

Another tip is to be aware of the fact that it is human nature to fidget, have labored breathing, or sweat profusely when nervous or frightened. The audible signs of movement and breathing can be detected. In order for you to be able to detect a suspect moving about, breathing heavily or fidgeting, you need to stop and listen frequently as you search a room or area.

Body odors can also be detected under the right circumstances. It is not an old wive's tale that fear can be smelled. Anyone who has ever been truly frightened can recall smelling their own body odors. This odor is simply an over secretion of adrenaline that is noticeable to the olfactory senses. For the search team to detect these things, they must move slowly and deliberately, stopping frequently, listening, and noting sound and odors while they conduct their search.

Don't get me wrong, I'm not telling you to stop and sniff the air like a canine, I am simply stating the fact that, under the right conditions, you may be able to smell body odors you normally wouldn't smell due to the suspect's fear, or even quite simply, from bad body odor due to filth or drug use.

Dealing with the Suspect

First, I want to emphasize what the search team should do when a suspect has been located:

- **DON'T RUSH** into anything!

    and

- **IDENTIFY** who you are!

P O L I C E - F R E E Z E!

or

S H E R I F F - F R E E Z E!

or

S E C U R I T Y - F R E E Z E!

Do this loudly and with authority.

I believe this accomplishes three things:

1. Your immediate challenge to the suspect to "Freeze" alerts your partner that a suspect has been located and eliminates the need for you to divert your attention from the suspect's location to get your partner's attention. This verbal challenge directs your partner's attention to where the suspect has been located eliminating the need for you to do so through additional verbalization or hand signals.

2. Immediate identification of who you are dispels any doubt in the suspect's mind that he is in fact being confronted by a law enforcement officer or security officer.

3. If there are citizens, other officers, or victims present when you are conducting the search, the loud command of identification negates the suspect's allegation that he didn't know who the officers were.

If the commands are given loud enough for the persons outside the building to hear them, then there is little room for doubt the suspects also heard you.

Second, I want to share some important officer safety reminders with you.

- **DON'T** jump into a confined area in an attempt to gain control over a suspect.

- Let the suspect do the work, make him move to an area of advantage to the officers.

- Always keep the suspect's hands in view.

- Always face the suspect away from the search team's position when tactically possible.

- Only one officer gives commands.

- Give clear, precise commands and directions to the suspect from a position of cover or concealment.

- Avoid crossfire situations by maintaining triangulation.

- The contact officer should holster and secure his weapon before making physical contact with the suspect.

- When tactically possible, control the suspect by hand-cuffing him immediately.

- After the suspect is handcuffed, always conduct a thorough search for weapons and other contraband.

- Always search the waist area first for weapons, and if the suspect is kneeling, search the ankle area as well.

- If a weapon is found it should be immediately verbalized "gun!"—"knife!" in a calm, commanding, and controlled voice.

- If weapons are found, secure them in your waistband, or if possible, in your pocket.

- Don't lay weapons on the floor or ground.

- If you can't secure them on your person, hand them off to your cover officer.

- Once the search is conducted, gather as much information as you can from the suspect; e.g., is there anyone else in the building? Is he armed? Where is he? Etc., etc.

Contact and Cover Officer

Contact Officer: The term "contact officer" identifies the officer who first located and challenged the suspect, and will eventually make physical contact with the suspect to handcuff and search him. Generally, the search officer makes contact with the suspect first, however it can be either the search officer or the cover officer who makes contact with the suspect, depending on the circumstances of the situation.

Search Officer Contact: To explain the contact officer's role, we will have the search officer locate the suspect, which now makes him the "contact officer." This officer gives all commands to the suspect, conducts the handcuff and search procedures, and maintains physical control of the suspect.

When the suspect is located, the officer immediately identifies himself and orders the suspect to put his hands in plain view. Commands to the suspect should be given from a position of cover or concealment. Besides the obvious reasons, the other benefit of using cover or concealment is to dissuade physical resistance to the arrest by the suspect because there is no clear path to the officer's position.

The suspect is immediately told to face away from the search team. He is directed to keep his hands in clear view, extended into the air with palms facing outward, or towards the search team. Once this is done, the suspect is directed to a location where the cover officer has a clear field-of-vision and an open field-of-fire, which allows the contact officer a safe approach to handcuff, search, and take the suspect into custody. The perimeter team is advised of the suspect contact when it is safe to do so. This can be done by the cover officer as soon as the suspect has been placed into a position of disadvantage, or once the suspect has been handcuffed and searched.

The contact officer should move in a manner which presents the least obstruction to the cover officer's line of sight and field-of-fire. Although there is no 100 percent safe way to conduct the handcuff and search procedure, by avoiding crossfire situations and sight obstructions of the cover officer, the safety of the contact officer is maximized. As previously mentioned, before making physical contact with the suspect, the contact officer should holster his weapon to permit two-handed control of the suspect. This lessens the chance of being disarmed if a physical confrontation takes place when actual contact is made with the suspect.

Cover Officer Contact: If the cover officer located the suspect, this officer then becomes the "contact officer." The search officer has now become the cover officer. There may be times when it is more tactically sound for the discovering officer to relinquish the role of contact officer when the contact officer's position does not allow him to assume a proper position of cover or concealment. These possibilities should be discussed and decided on when entry and search plans are devised. This is an excellent example of what complementing each other means, being able to transition smoothly, the roles of the search team from one to the other without conscious effort.

Cover Officer: When a suspect has been located, the cover officer's position should be behind cover or concealment, presenting the least chance of a crossfire situation. He should have an unobstructed line-of-vision to the suspect, with an open field-of-fire in case the suspect is armed and resorts to a lethal confrontation or some form of physical resistance. The cover officer does not give commands to the suspect or have physical contact with him during this procedure. If the contact officer is physically unable to control the suspect, then the cover officer needs to assist in controlling the suspect. The possibility of a suspect resisting arrest should be discussed in the planning stages of your search. There should be an agreed upon "key" word or phrase used by the contact officer that will trigger the cover officer to move in and physically assist the contact officer in controlling the suspect. The cover officer's weapon should be holstered and secured before assisting the control officer.

Moving The Suspect: Once the suspect has been controlled, handcuffed and searched, if it has not already been done, notify the perimeter team a suspect has been located and is in custody. Now comes the tricky part, how is the suspect to be removed from the building? Since most agencies don't have the luxury of spare officers, we must proceed on the assumption there are only two members on the entry team and a limited number of perimeter officers, generally only one or two.

So, do both officers take the suspect out of the building? Does one officer stay inside while the other takes the suspect out? Can members of the perimeter team enter and take control of the suspect? Well, all three of the tactics mentioned are acceptable. These options should have been discussed thoroughly when the entry and search plans were conceived. Regardless of the method employed, communication between officers is imperative when moving the suspect out of the building. Let's take a look at the three options presented.

Option One: (One-in—One-out) This option leaves one team member inside the building to maintain the integrity of the search while the other team member removes the suspect from the building. The theory is that once ground is gained, it is not given up. The officer who remains inside the building would normally be designated the control and containment officer, while the contact officer removes the suspect from the building.

The control and containment officer should take a position of cover or concealment with his back to the area just searched, focusing his attention on the area forward of his position, and control the un-searched areas by dominating them with his weapon. The officer should take as comfortable a position as possible, control his breathing, remain quiet, avoid moving about, and look and listen to what is going on inside the building. This option compromises officer safety to a degree because one member of the search team is left alone inside the building.

When a captured suspect is being removed, additional suspects in the building may believe the officers have left the building, and may leave their places of concealment. If this were to happen, the control and containment officer should notify the perimeter team and his partner of the situation. If suspect contact is unavoidable, the control and containment officer must act on his own. The officer identifies himself then verbally controls the suspects by having them place their hands in clear view, and turn away from the officer's position, placing them in a position of disadvantage, or place them into a prone position, arms extended outward with their palms up. Keep as much distance between the suspects and the control and containment officer as tactically possible while maintaining physical control of the suspect by holding them at gunpoint. The officer should not approach the suspects until assistance has arrived. Once assistance has arrived, the handcuff and search procedures are followed.

Whenever a suspect is being taken from the building, a running dialogue with the perimeter team is maintained as the officer and suspect move through the building, exiting the building at the same location the search team entered. This dialogue is also monitored by the control and containment officer. Once clear of the building a member of the perimeter team takes control of the suspect from the contact officer as soon as possible. When re-entry is made, a running dialogue between the contact officer and the control and containment officer is maintained until the two officers are once again together as the search and cover officers.

Option Two: (Two-out) This option has both members of the search team exiting the building with the suspect. If this option is used, the perimeter team is notified immediately that both members of the search team will be exiting the building with the suspect. As with Option One, when the suspect is being taken from the building, a running dialogue with the perimeter team is maintained by the cover officer as the officers and suspect move through the building, exiting the building at the same location the search team entered. Once outside, a member of the perimeter team takes control of the suspect from the control officer as soon as possible.

The perimeter team must be extra alert as the search

team is moving through the building with the suspect. The search team's movements can easily cover the sounds of additional suspects moving through the building. With a suspect in custody, the search team is generally unable to move in a stealth mode as they move through the building and exit. If members of the perimeter team are not alert to this fact, additional suspects could escape or one of the search team members could be falsely identified as a suspect and be injured or killed by a fellow officer. Furthermore, a member of the perimeter team could easily be injured or killed by the unexpected presence of an escaping suspect.

The major problem with this option is that once the officers have left the building, the entire search has been compromised. The building must now be searched a second time from the point of entry to the location where the suspect was found. The inherent problem is that the search team becomes complacent during the second search through the same territory. Officers often fail to consider the fact that additional suspects may have relocated in an attempt to escape. The suspects may believe the officers won't search the same area again and when the officers leave, they will be able to escape, which creates a safety hazard for the officers. However, the greatest safety hazard is that other suspects in the building could easily ambush the officers, either while they are exiting the building, because their focus has been diverted to the suspect they have in custody, or when they re-enter the building.

I believe this option creates too many additional officer safety hazards. I do not recommend using this option because of the inherent officer safety issues it presents. It is very time consuming and this, in-and-of itself, creates additional safety hazards. Using one of the other options presented, significantly reduces these hazards.

Option Three: (Two-in. One or Two- in and out) This option leaves both team members inside the building to maintain the integrity of the search, because additional officers present at the scene can be used to remove the suspect. This is the best of the three options for officer safety, search integrity, and suspect control. As in Option One, the theory is that once ground is gained, it is not given up. One or two of the perimeter officers enter the building to take control of the suspect. The officers can be identified as "custody officers" for ease of understanding their role.

The custody officers enter at the same location the search team entered. A running dialogue is maintained with the search team as the custody officers move through the building to meet up with the search team. The dialogue lets the search team know where the custody officers are, and from what direction they are approaching the search team. They enter and move in a tactical manner, as though they were the search team, keeping in mind that additional suspects may still be present in the building. Additional suspects could use the custody officers' movements to mask their own movements in an attempt to escape.

The custody officers remove the suspect from the building. Again, a running dialogue is maintained with the perimeter team as they move back through the building until they exit with the suspect. The exit point is the same location at which they entered. The search team resumes searching the building once the custody officers have advised them they are clear of the building.

What should you do with the suspect if there aren't any perimeter officers, or there is only one perimeter officer blocking the most likely escape route? There are few options available. You can't have the sole perimeter officer leave his position, so the only alternative would be for the contact officer to place the suspect in the back seat of the closest unit to the perimeter officer. This permits some control over the suspect by the perimeter officer. If there is no perimeter officer, the contact officer would have to place the suspect in the back seat of the closest unit to the entry point. No matter what the situation, the suspect is always handcuffed to the rear, handcuffs double locked, and the suspect secured in the unit with the seat belt. An additional option to help secure the suspect is to loop the handcuffs through a belt or belt loop behind the suspect's back if available. I don't like the idea of leaving a suspect unattended in a patrol unit; however, real life options aren't always the best.

Post Arrest Intelligence: No matter which option is used, once a suspect is removed from the building, intelligence information must be gathered. Ask the suspect if there are additional persons inside the building, who they are, where they are, are they armed, and armed with what? This questioning is in furtherance of an investigation and is not a violation of Miranda. If a member of the search team is not present when this questioning is done, then the information is immediately communicated to them.

A word of caution! If the suspect says there is no one else inside the building, you must exercise extreme caution not to become complacent while completing the search. You must remain alert and search with the thought that additional suspects are still in the building. **Remember, suspects do lie!**

Suspect Search Reminders: ALWAYS search any suspect you are taking custody of from another officer. In December of 2003 a California Sheriff's Department had a suspect in custody for shooting a deputy sheriff. The suspect was placed in an interview room, without being handcuffed. Officers came in and out of the room, at times turning their back to the suspect. After giving the suspect a bottle of water, an officer walked out of the interview room leaving the suspect unattended. Within seconds after the officer left the room, the suspect took a .45 caliber pistol from his left front pocket and shot himself in the head. The officers who took custody of him from another agency had NOT searched the suspect. There are many lessons to be learned from this, however the most important is to ALWAYS conduct your own search of suspects, regardless of who you took custody of the suspects from, or under what circumstances you took custody of them.

CHAPTER 9
THE NUMBERING SYSTEM

SWAT-teams use a numbering and lettering system to identify the sides of a building, and in multiple story buildings, the floors of those buildings. The system simplifies identification of perimeter placement with numbers assigned to the front, sides, and back of the building in place of compass directions. As with other SWAT concepts, there is no reason why patrol officers can't adopt this methodology as well to aid them in setting perimeters at building searches. The system was conceived because confusion often arose over compass directions which have, on more than one occasion, created officer safety hazards and allowed suspects to escape.

The system is easily used and understood. Although it is a two-part system of numbering and lettering, normally only the numbering system is needed by a patrol force that will be searching a building.

The numerical assignments run clockwise, or left to right.

#1 is the FRONT of the building, or what is designated as the *main* entrance.

#2 is the LEFT side of the building.

#3 is the BACK of the building.

#4 is the RIGHT side of the building.

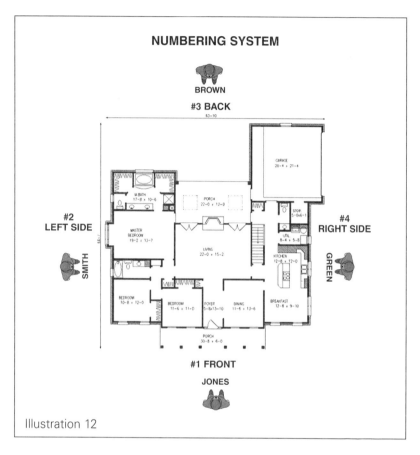

Illustration 12

As a further explanation of the system, let's take a situation and place officers on the perimeter.

Officer Jones is positioned on the ONE SIDE. (Front)

Officer Smith is positioned on the TWO SIDE. (Left)

Officer Brown is positioned on the THREE SIDE. (Back)

Officer Green is positioned on the FOUR SIDE. (Right)

These positions are easy to relate to and identify. Jones is on the front. Smith is on the left side. Brown is on the back. Green is on the right side.

In line with the fact we probably won't have four officers to set up an inner perimeter, we will have to use a two-officer Diagonal Perimeter. officer Green is placed at the ONE and FOUR (1-4) corner, and is responsible for the ONE and FOUR sides. Officer Smith is placed on the TWO and THREE (2-3) corner, and is responsible for the TWO and THREE sides. Even though this isn't the ideal perimeter, the officers can effectively cover potential escape routes.

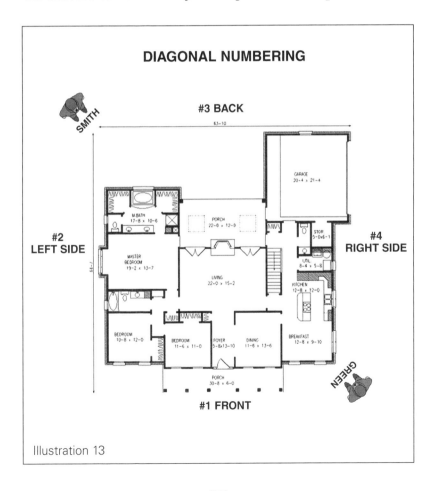

Illustration 13

With a little practice and perseverance, you can simplify setting perimeters at building searches and other tactical situations by knowing how to properly apply this numbering system. When the situation requires knowing the positions of officers, the numbering system can be used in open area perimeters, on grid searches, outer perimeters, sealing off buildings, rooms, etc., etc.

Alpha (Floor) Identification System: Generally, this system applies to commercial buildings of three floors or more, but can be used on residential buildings as well. The floors are identified with an alphabetical (alpha) designator. Starting with the letter "A" assigned to the first visible bottom floor, with each floor assigned the consecutive alpha letter, extending upward to the top floor. The basement, or below ground floors, are generally not assigned a letter, but are referred to as such, i.e., basement.

Multiple story building searches require each floor to be divided into sectors, or quadrants, which are then numbered for identification. The search teams are then divided accordingly and the search is conducted as described in Chapter 10.

NOTE: Some agencies designate the top floor as "A" and extend down to the visible bottom floor, excluding the basement, or sub-floors. If this method is used, all involved officers must be aware of it.

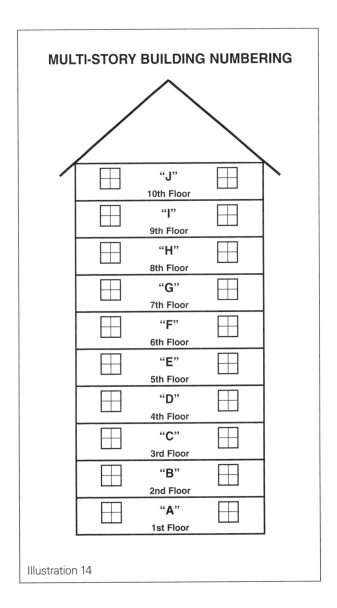

Illustration 14

CHAPTER 10
MULTIPLE STORY BUILDINGS

Multiple story buildings present unusual and unique problems for the patrol officer. Keeping in mind that agency policy will dictate much of what is done in multiple story building searches, i.e., who will conduct them, what patrol's role will be, etc., there are some general guidelines and information you should know so you will have a better understanding of the complexities of conducting such a search. However, regardless of the type of building being searched, the same basic officer safety and search practices are followed, i.e. clearing avenues of approach, setting inner and outer perimeters, etc. Generally, commercial buildings of three stories or more are considered to be multiple story buildings and are normally searched by multiple search teams. However, two, three or even four story residential dwellings normally don't fall into this category, and are usually searched by a standard search team; ergo, two or more patrol officers that comprise a search team.

Basic Methodology: Ideally, multiple story buildings are searched from the top down. An "interior" inner perimeter may be needed. This is accomplished by having a team enter the building to secure a safe operating zone so that the elevators and escalators (if any) are cleared, shut down, and secured on the first floor of the building if possible, and all avenues of escape are secured and blocked. If there is a basement in the building, it is secured by closing off the access points and posting officers to guard them. This is the last floor to be searched. A helicopter can be used to put a point team and perimeter officers on the roof to clear and secure the top floor access points. If this is not possible, fire escapes or stairways are cleared and secured from the ground floor to the top floor by using a point team to lead the other teams and perimeter officers from floor to floor.

As the point team begins to clear the access points, they must consider noise, the element of surprise, and the fact the suspect or suspects, may be trying to escape by using the same access points the point teams are moving through to clear. As the point team clears the fire escapes or stairways, a perimeter officer is positioned at the access points on each floor. Generally, there are a minimum of two sets of fire escapes in most commercial buildings. However, depending on the size of the building and its construction, there may be multiple fire escapes that need to be secured to prevent escape or double back by a suspect or suspects. These need to be secured the same as the other fire escapes, by posting perimeter officers at each level, even though these access points are not being used by the search teams.

The search teams will be using these access points to move between floors, transport suspects up or down, etc. Once the top floor of the building has been searched and secured, you may want to consider using one elevator to bring the remainder of the teams and their equipment to the top floor, if they haven't followed the point team up.

When tactically possible, all search teams enter the floor to be searched at the same entry point. No team moves to another floor until all teams are ready to move. Once the floor is cleared, the perimeter officers remain at the access points until the entire building has been searched and cleared. If there is a critical manpower shortage, the floors can be secured by blocking off or locking the access point doors. If a fire escape door is also an access point, locking it will not prevent someone inside from getting outside. The doors are equipped with a "panic bar", i.e., a push bar on the inside that overrides the lock to allow people to escape in an emergency.

Canine Teams: Part of the overall tactical plan will normally include the use of canine teams. Canine teams should have definitive search assignments to avoid creating hazards and conflict with other search teams. They may be assigned to a particular team, placed on stand-by until needed, or assigned their own area to search. Regardless of how the canine is used, they should be used conservatively, based on the size of the building to be searched. Canines tire easily in an extensive search environment, therefore, their use should be well thought out before committing them to "just search." To avoid misuse of the canine and its capabilities, you should discuss their use and capabilities with the handler(s) prior to including them in the search plan and, of course, agency policy or practices need to be a part of this discussion.

Intelligence Information: Multiple search teams require detailed briefings, planning, and a tactical command post from which to operate. Because of the complexities in a multiple story search, the search teams need all the intelligence information they can get. Aside from suspect information, this information should include floor schematics which show all aspects of each floor being searched, such as crawl spaces, air conditioning ducts, vents, telephone switching rooms, electrical control panels or rooms, furnace and/or boiler rooms, sprinkler controls and valves, hazards, light switches, security monitors, security mirrors, offices, hallways, break rooms, bathrooms, etc.

Keys for doors and access ways should be provided to each search team. If there are insufficient keys for each team, then keys should be made. This enhances officer safety and makes the search easier, while eliminating the need to breach doors by forcing them open and lessening the potential damage caused by breaching.

The Search Teams: Search teams can be comprised of 2, 4, 6, 8, etc., or however many the supervisor deems necessary, plus a team leader. They are each assigned a name designator, such as Alpha Team, Bravo Team, Charlie Team, Delta Team, Echo Team, etc., for identification. By having definitive identifiers, confusion about assignments is avoided.

Each team is assigned specific sectors to search. For example, Alpha Team will search Sector One, Bravo Team will search Sector Two, Charlie Team will search Sector Three, Delta Team will search Sector Four, Echo Team will search Sector Five, etc.

Communication: Because of the large number of personnel involved multiple radio channels will have to be used. One primary channel is assigned to the operation for the tactical commander to communicate between dispatch and the command post, if one is used. Tactical channels are assigned to the search teams, and perimeter personnel. The tactical commander will generally be too busy with his operational planning to monitor all of the radio channels. A dispatcher or officer is assigned to monitor the primary channel and additional dispatchers or officers are assigned to monitor the tactical channels, each being respnsible to keep the tactical commander apprised of what is happening with each team and the perimeter. The use of multiple radio channels is usually necessary when there are three or more teams searching. If only two teams are searching, the operation could be conducted using a primary channel for all communication between dispatch and the tactical commander as well as the search teams and perimeter personnel. Regardless of how many teams there are, or how many radio channels are used, radio discipline is a must.

Once the search starts, communication should be between search team leaders and search team members, in limited transmissions, and with search team leaders and the tactical command post for situational updates, when a suspect has been located, when additional equipment is needed, when coordinating team movement from floor-to-floor, or when a team may need assistance.

Documenting the Search: A check-off list is maintained at the tactical command post as the search progresses, identifying the search teams, floor, and search sectors. The check-off list is a chronological log of the search and its results, such as arrests (where, when, and how many), which floors have been cleared and secured, etc. Of course, agency policy and practice will dictate how you document this type of search. I believe the check-off list is one of the easiest methods to use for documenting these types of searches.

Manpower Use: As stated before, multiple story building searches are normally done using patrol officers as search teams because of the high manpower needs. These searches are only extensions of the many searches you will do as a part of your daily duties. You should not hesitate to call for assistance when faced with a multiple story-building search. For you to attempt a search of this magnitude with a two-person search team is foolish.

CHAPTER 11
TACTICAL DIAGRAMMING

The term "Tactical Diagramming" was originated by then Lieutenant Sid Heal of the Los Angeles County (CA) Sheriff's Department. Now a Captain, Sid is one of this nation's foremost authorities on tactical applications for SWAT and patrol officers. He has written a book on the subject of tactical diagramming, *Tactical Diagramming Hints,* published by Varro Press and offers classes on its application. I highly recommend you purchase his book and attend his class.

I use Sid's terminology because it best describes what an officer is trying to accomplish by applying the principles of residential construction to law enforcement use. I have taken my own experiences in the construction trade, coupled with some basic research in the recent trends of residential construction, to give you the information that follows; addressing residential construction practices, in particular building code requirements that provide us with tactical information. With this information you can learn to "read" a house.

Almost every time we respond to a call where a building search is the end result, the building itself is an unknown to us. Basically, this means that we don't know what the floor plan is. This is true whether it's a residential dwelling or commercial building. Because of these unknowns, officer safety concerns become critical when the patrol officer is setting up a search team and planning a building entry and search. Even though the search team has devised a tactical plan prior to entry, in reality, the search team is almost "blind" until they make entry and begin moving through the building. It's only then that they can begin to apply their tactical plan based on what they are confronted with as they move through the building.

Because most commercial buildings differ from floor to floor and present construction concepts that go from basic building principles to futuristic designs, it is next to impossible to try and figure out floor plans of each floor using the "tactical diagramming" theory, which only reinforces the principles discussed in Chapter 10 on multiple story building searches.

Conversely, construction requirements for residential dwellings remain fairly consistent even with ultra-modern or futuristic designs. It is this consistency which affords us the opportunity to apply the tactical diagramming theory.

Over the years, SWAT officers have learned to "read" a residential dwelling and devise some type of tactical diagram that provides a basic floor plan of the dwelling. It is my belief that patrol officers should be able to do the same thing when confronted with an unknown building search.

Therefore, tactical diagramming is looking at the outside of a residence and devising a floor plan based on doors, windows, walls, knowledge of basic construction trends in floor plan designs, interior decorations visible through windows, roof construction, roof vents and other factors. There are some construction similarities between commercial and residential dwellings that will also be discussed.

Keep it Safe and Simple: When the residence to be searched is located in a housing tract and the availability of looking at a house with the same floor plan as the one to be searched is presented, KISS it, keep it safe and simple by taking advantage of the opportunity. If the house has a reverse floor plan, sketch it, then reverse it to match the house you will be searching. And when neighbors or other persons are present, ask for assistance, they may able to provide you with a floor plan of the residence or give you other information about the residence that may help you plan your search. At the very least their information can be used to corroborate the information you gathered based on the tactical diagramming theories.

Construction Transitions: People and their habits have dictated how homes have been constructed over the years based on their need, or lack of need, for privacy. A little known fact about the construction of homes is the transition that home designs and floor plans have taken over the years. For example, homes built in the early part of the last century up through the late 1960's and early 1970's were built with open construction concepts. People were more friendly and trusting, and more open and friendly with their neighbors. Therefore, living areas were in the front of the home, front porches were common and large windows in the living areas faced the street. Bedrooms were more often in the back portion of the house. Somewhere around the mid 1970's to early 1980's, homes became less open in construction. People became less friendly and open. They became more private and less interactive with their neighbors. Today, people keep more to themselves to the point that few people even know or speak to their neighbors. Because of this trend, front porches where people would visit and gather are becoming a thing of the past, living areas have been moved away from the street to the back part of the home, with larger windows in the living areas facing private areas of the property, such as back yards and side yards. Bedrooms are now more often in the front portion of the house.

These construction trends are not absolutes, but are general trends provided to assist you in identifying some newer and older home constructions. As you continue to learn about residential construction trends and designs, apply this knowledge in such a manner that it will assist you in your tactical plans for conducting a building search.

Home Designs: Generally, homes are designed and separated into three areas; living, eating, and sleeping. This does not mean that they are restricted to these areas alone. Keep in mind that home design and construction are based on the desires of the owner or builder. For example, custom homes may include a separation of more than one living area into recreation areas, such as game rooms or home offices, and there may be more than one primary sleeping area, one for family members and one designated solely for guests. This principle also applies to tract homes where they are built in phases and the owners are able to make modifications to the basic floor plan.

Below is the breakdown of what is generally contained within a particular area:

- *Living areas:*

   Living room.

   Television room.

   Family room.

   Den or game room.

   Home office.

- *Eating areas:*

   Kitchen.

   Dining room.

   Breakfast nook.

   Formal dining areas.

- *Sleeping areas:*

   Normally off of living areas and next to each other, generally not near food areas.

   Bedrooms, including master bedroom.

   Guest rooms.

   Lofts used as sleeping areas

Construction Norms: The majority of all homes have the same construction principles for walls, windows, bathrooms, bedrooms, venting, electrical, etc. To keep this information from running together, I will talk about each construction principle separately.

Walls: Exterior walls are usually constructed of stucco, brick, block, stone, or wood. Exterior walls can be hollow, depending on their construction material. Interior walls are normally hollow and constructed of sheet rock, lath and plaster, or wood. There could be sound barriers between sleeping and living areas, such as bathrooms, closets, and stairwells. Other sound barriers could be walls with foam or other materials placed between the studs, or put under the primary wall material.

All homes have barrier and bearing walls. The barrier walls discussed here are not to be confused with sound barrier walls, which generally do not carry any type of weight load. Barrier walls support the roofline. Depending on the design of the home, there could be more than one barrier wall. Generally the barrier wall runs through the center of the home. Outer walls are bearing walls, meaning that the roof is supported by them too. In multi-story homes, the barrier walls run top to bottom through all floors. Hallways are generally along barrier and bearing walls; inner hallways, center of home, outer hallways, along outside walls.

Windows: The windows in most homes will generally tell the officer what the rooms are. Area windows are normally placed in the center of the wall, generally these are in living areas. Most building codes require that 1/8th of a room must have window glass. Based on this fact, you should be able to estimate the approximate size of the room, and a general indication where the walls are located. The formula for this is to measure the width of the glass, divide it by 20 and multiply by 100.

Eating area windows are fairly distinctive. Kitchen windows are normally located over a sink, or at or near a corner and are usually narrower and slightly higher than other windows. Some kitchen windows may be located in the center of the wall. Dining areas may have windows and/or sliding glass doors, French doors, or atrium doors. Door coverings in dining areas are generally traverse drapes, or horizontal blinds.

Bedroom windows are normally higher than living area windows, usually 3' to 4' from the ground. Bedroom windows can be at one end of the room, or in the center of the room. A small translucent window near the bedroom window indicates the presence of a bathroom, which may also identify the master bedroom. Another indicator of a bedroom is the type of curtains in the window. Bedroom curtains are generally ruffled and more elegant than those in other areas of the home.

Living area windows are slightly lower than sleeping area windows. Usually 3' above the ground. They are normally the largest windows in the house. Some living areas have cape cod style windows, French doors, atrium doors, or sliding doors. Normally traverse drapes that open at the middle, or from the right or left side are used on living area windows. If there are doors in the living area, such as sliding doors, French doors, or atrium doors, they may be covered using traverse drapes or horizontal blinds.

Bathroom windows are normally the highest window in the house and are smaller than any other window in the house. They are usually translucent, frosted, or glass blocks, which prevent people from looking in through the window from the outside. These types of windows located on outer walls away from a bedroom would indicate the bathroom is off of a hallway. When located on the end of the house, it would indicate it is either at the end of a hallway, or could be off of a master bedroom. Bathroom windows generally do not have curtains or blinds, however, this is not always the case. Window coverings could be vinyl or other water resistant material, usually with some type of bright colors, aquatic design or floral designs.

Doors: Generally, exterior residential doors open inward and are solid core. Exterior doors are a minimum of 36" wide. They can vary upward in width, if they are custom built or double doors. Most often the right door on a set of double doors is the operational door. All homes must have two exterior doors, that must be on opposite sides of the house. Front doors can be extremely fancy, or simple in design. Construction can be wood, metal, hardboard, or fabricated material. In older homes, doors leading into the residence from the garage can be either hollow core or solid core. In newer homes they can be either hollow core or a solid core fire resistant door.

Interior doors can be 26", 28" or 30" wide. Generally bedroom doors are 26" or 28" wide and bathroom and closet doors are 24" or 26" wide. Interior doors normally open into a room against a wall, with the light switch on the knob side of the door. Normally the largest part of the room will be away from the hinged side of the door. Interior doors are almost always hollow core and are either wood or hardboard. Doors that close off hallways could be a solid core, fire resistant door. Fire resistant doors can be found in any residential structure, however they are generally found in custom-built homes, or homes built to be board and care homes, or a home that has been remodeled for some special use requiring fire resistant doors as a part of the building code.

Roof Vents: Roof vents are comprised of two basic types: combustion and water vents. Combustion vents are for gas appliances and usually have an umbrella. They are located at or near an exterior wall and normally indicate the kitchen and hot water heater. In older homes, the hot water heater is located in or close to the kitchen. In newer homes it is located in the garage or laundry area. The vent nearest the center of the home generally indicates the kitchen.

Water appliance vents are usually galvanized or PVC pipe, 1" to 2" in diameter, extending approximately 12" above the roof line without a cover. These vents are for sinks and toilets in bathrooms, kitchen sinks, and laundry areas. Usually bathrooms are next to each other. Two story homes usually have the bathrooms on top of each other and run off the same vent pipes.

To Create a Floor Plan: Locate the stove vent to identify the location of the kitchen area. Off of the kitchen will be the dining area, moving right or left from the dining area will be the living areas, then sleeping areas which are usually on the opposite side of the house from the living areas. This information, coupled with identifying windows, doors, and other vent pipe locations, should give you a rough idea of the floor plan.

Construction Tips

The following information addresses commercial and residential construction norms that will provide you with the basic knowledge of doors and light switches to aid you with your tactical diagramming capabilities.

Commercial Doors: Commercial building codes are specific as to escape means for fire safety. Because of this, commercial buildings in the past 25 years or so have had to comply with these codes. Exterior doors in commercial buildings must open out with a fire bar or fire handle on the inside. They must be a minimum of 36" wide, and be solid core or metal. Interior doors are also 36" wide and usually open into the room, but in older buildings may open out into the hallway or entry way. On some older buildings, exterior doors may open inward without any means of emergency escape provisions.

Light Switches: In residential dwellings, the light switches may vary in height, but are normally at the same height throughout the dwelling, generally 42" to 46" above the floor, and are normally located on the knob side of the door. On rare occasions, generally in older homes, the light switch may be on the opposite wall from which the door opens.

In commercial buildings, the light switches are normally at the same height throughout the building, 42" above the floor, and located on the knob side of the door. In some military installations and older buildings, they can be in three different locations. On the opposite wall from which the door opens, on the opposite wall the door opens away from or in the middle of the wall, across from where the door opens.

Although I haven't talked about all aspects of building construction, such as the many types of roofs that would indicate more than one barrier wall that can help you determine additional rooms or stories, or other exterior indicators of rooms, such as gables, dormers, etc.; the information provided will give you a head start on how to use tactical diagramming to your advantage.

Remember, even though home construction is fairly consistent, changes are constantly being made in building codes, building materials, floor plans, and the way people want their homes to be built. For example, there is a very large construction company building large and small housing tracts, custom homes, and commercial buildings throughout the United States. They offer over 10,000 personal modifications to the custom and tract homes they build. That's right, ten thousand! The modifications can be as simple as paint schemes to floor plan designs, to realignment of the living, eating, and sleeping areas that may or may not fit the norm.

Nothing is truly constant. Change is always present. In the instance of residential and commercial building construction, these changes will always impact you when you have to conduct a building search. The point is, don't take construction trends and building codes as absolutes. Always be aware of changes. Look for them when planning your entry and search tactics and devising your tactical diagrams.

And finally, you need to practice "reading" a house. Start with your own home, or go to a housing tract. Complete your tactical diagram then compare it with the floor plans. The more homes you do, the more proficient you become. Eventually your tactical diagrams will be extremely accurate, giving you an advantage you didn't have before.

CHAPTER 12
SUMMARY

Building searches will always be among the most dangerous assignments you will face. It is my intent with this book, to raise your level of awareness by providing you with a working knowledge and understanding of how to conduct building searches with minimal risk to yourself and your partner. As I stated early on, this book is not a panacea for all building search situations and should be used as a guideline to strengthen your own skills and talents.

The philosophies, concepts, tactics, and techniques presented in this book are a compilation of experiences I have gained over the years and by officers with whom I have worked and/or trained. There is no 100 percent safe way to search a building. You must always remember that your safety comes first. If you do not protect yourself from harms way, no one will. Before responding to and handling any type of call, you should have some type of tactical plan in mind. You should think about what you are doing, how you are going to do it, and with whom. The most dangerous thing you can let happen to yourself is to let your mind become lazy and not think about officer safety.

Your safety in a building search is contingent upon how well you understand the dynamics of a building search, coupled with your personal skills and abilities. If you have taken every precaution preparing for the search, have the right mental attitude, and are secure in your knowledge, you will be able to safely complete the search.

But always remember, Mr. Murphy seems to come along for the ride no matter how well we plan.

I want to emphasize the importance of keeping your planning and tactics simple. I have learned from years of experience, as have others, that the more complicated the plans and tactics, the more likely something will go wrong. Building your entry tactics and plans around "Safe and Simple" will almost always present the most viable plan of action. The more simple the plan the easier it is for everyone to understand and successfully execute, be it a SWAT entry or a building search by patrol officers. However, always be prepared to adapt, improvise and overcome.

**Ambivalence, complacency, and boredom
are an officer's worst enemies.**

Do not let these enemies interfere with your ability to make rational, safe decisions, regardless of the situation.

**Don't let ambivalence, complacency, and
boredom be your epitaph!**

Be safe and go home!

CHAPTER 13
BRAVING THE NEW WORLD

In the years since I started writing this book, many things have changed in the world that have directly affected our profession. The premise of this book is to give you some insight about how to conduct a safe building search, and to instill in you the need to always practice officer safety tactics and techniques above and beyond what ever else you do.

This final chapter reflects my personal thoughts and feelings about what is going on in our country and the world today, and how these events will impact you and me as cops; they are not politically correct! I have always held that the truth sometimes hurts, and the only way to convey a message with clarity is to say it without the hindrance of political correctness. My comments are not intended to offend, defame, or denounce anyone, nor are they intended to infer that any one person, group, or profession is solely accountable for what is happening in our world today. I simply want you to know that your job is becoming increasingly more dangerous, with higher expectations of "perfection," but with no real expectation of support from your own upper management, the media and some of the very people you have sworn to protect and serve.

On September 11, 2001, the cowardly attack on America created a new threat that law enforcement was not fully prepared to deal with at all. And now, years later, we are still not fully prepared to deal with this threat as effectively as we should be. Looking back over the days, weeks, and months after 9-11, I recall that our department received an overwhelming number of calls about suspicious packages, suspicious persons of Middle Eastern descent, letters believed to be contaminated with anthrax, and a host of other fears about things the general public thought might be terrorist related. It got so bad the airlines removed powdered cream and sugar packages from their galleys because people believed they might be anthrax, and they quit serving in-flight meals with silverware and other utensils they were afraid could be used as weapons. Even though the overwhelming majority of citizen calls were unfounded, the mere reporting of all the calls and the new security measure enacted created fear, panic, and paranoia – some of the primary goals of the terrorist.

The potential for more terrorist attacks against America and Americans is real, inside our borders and worldwide. Attacks inside our borders will be handled by law enforcement in our role as first responders. These compelling factors are why I have added some basic information about how terrorists operate: to help prepare you to respond to calls with the thought in mind that any call could very well be a terrorist attack.

You are already keenly aware that you will be called on many times as a law enforcement officer to go in harms way. Today you are faced with a society that is becoming more and more violent. In spite of the fact that today there are more than 60,000 gun control laws, several hundred laws addressing domestic violence, and numerous other laws pertaining to rape, robbery and other violent crimes, none of these laws seem to deter criminals from doing what they do. Add to these, the fact that the threat of life in prison for "three strikers" and career criminals doesn't mean a thing to these people, just as the death penalty is no deterrent to those who commit murder.

An undeniable symptom of the culture of violence that has permeated our society is the skyrocketing incidence of officer-involved shootings and assaults on officers. Did you know that over 60,000 officers are assaulted yearly; ironically this coincides with the same number of ineffective gun control laws. The number of these assaults has remained fairly constant for over five years. Is there a message here? I think so! Controlling guns doesn't do a damn thing, controlling criminals who use guns, does. Other indicators of this increased violence is the need to construct more jails— federal, state, and local—to house those convicted of criminal acts, be they a violent crime, narcotics, theft, or whatever; our jails are full. I believe these factors support my position that people today, for the most part, have lost respect for the law and those who enforce it.

Proof of my thesis is that the term "active shooter" has now been added to the law enforcement lexicon. We call these people "active shooters" because, with premeditation and planning, they carry out their indiscriminate acts of violence with deliberate intentions. They have horrified the nation with their senseless and mindless assaults, using firearms and explosives against their friends, classmates, and teachers in the schools they attend. However, the active shooter is not limited to school violence, there are adults who kill simply because they are angry with their boss or co-workers, or don't like the color of a person's skin, their religion, or their nationality. Quite often active shooters refuse to accept responsibility for their criminal acts. Instead, they try to justify their actions with some lame excuse that they were not liked or accepted by their peers, or their parents, co-workers, friends, or society as a whole failed to "understand" them.

I'm not a psychologist or psychiatrist, so I can't give you any scientific or medical reasons why these people do what they do and it wouldn't matter if I could. But I do know that when these atrocities are committed, you and I will be the ones who will be called on to respond to them. We will be expected to control them, and rightfully so. Even though these incidents greatly increase the probability of us suffering great bodily harm or even death, we willingly go in harms way to do what we are sworn to do, protect and serve. We are all concerned and fear for our own safety, the safety of our fellow officers, and the safety of the public, but we put aside our fear so we can perform our sworn duties, and generally we don't verbalize these feelings to those outside our profession.

Remember, society as a whole doesn't know or understand what we actually do and why we do it. They are unaware that we may face life and death situations on an almost daily basis in our careers; that we have been confronted by some creep who just committed a petty crime and wants to kill us to avoid being arrested; that some dirt bag wants to kill us just because we're cops. Society fails to realize that we see death, violence, and man's inhumanity to man almost every day. They have no clue as to the unusually high amount of social pressures, anxieties, and stressors that are placed on us because of these factors. I am not complaining about this lack of knowledge, I am just stating a fact. The truth of the matter is this, the average person in our society will never really know or fully understand what we do and go through because they will never see or experience what we do. Because society does not know these things, or fails to recognize and acknowledge our willingness to face these dangers in order to protect and serve them, is not a factor that our critics will consider.

We are often second guessed and criticized for not responding fast enough, or failing to take what is perceived to be the proper action. And when deadly force is used we are criticized for not "just wounding" the person who started the mayhem. Society in general dismisses the dangers and problems these incidents present to law enforcement and other public safety officers because they believe "that's what you get paid to do." In reality, this criticism shifts the blame for violence and mayhem to law enforcement, instead of the person or persons who deliberately initiate these senseless acts. Because we are professional law enforcement officers we listen to our critics, and sometimes we benefit from it. When the criticism is not constructive or warranted, we move on, never failing to accept our responsibilities as law enforcement officers to protect and serve the people, even our critics. In my 38 plus years in law enforcement I can count on one hand the times a criminal actually took responsibility for their actions without blaming society or someone else first. Cops don't.

Since the inception of the term active shooter, almost every law enforcement agency in the nation has developed some type of response protocol. I address the active shooter phenomena primarily because of the mind-set and intention these persons all seem to have in common: kill as many people as they can before killing themselves, being killed, or giving up. These people should not be classified as criminals, but as domestic terrorists because their purpose, aside from killing people, is to create fear, panic and paranoia, therefore their mind-set is the same as the international or state sponsored terrorist. Since 9-11 most agencies are still struggling with a protocol to deal with potential terrorist activities; other than bomb calls, biological threats and/or hazardous material spills, or suspected chemical agents. My goal is not to present you with a protocol, per se, but to cause you to think and prepare yourself to respond to a potential active shooter scene, a bomb threat, or other similar incident with the thought in mind that things may not be what they seem, and recognize that any incident could, in fact, be an act of terrorism.

Terrorism has been around for centuries, mostly in what we refer to as "third world" countries. It had never really been a threat to the United States, until September 11, 2001. In 2004, intelligence agencies estimated that upwards of 30,000 terrorists had been trained in various camps throughout the world prior to 9-11 and that since 9-11 the number of terrorists has steadily increased. There is a former Democratic presidential candidate who publicly stated in 2004 that terrorism should be reduced to a "nuisance," therefore I can only presume that he really believes this. I can say with certainty sir, that you are wrong! Terrorism should never be considered a nuisance. Terrorists kill masses of innocent people and perform public beheadings in an effort to force compliance with their demands or beliefs. Believing they can act with impunity, terrorists destroy countless lives, cities, and countries. Terrorism will never be just a "nuisance" Mr. Kerry! The truth is that terrorism is a barbaric and unacceptable behavior that must be stopped, no matter what it takes.

Almost every identified terrorist involved in the attacks on America had some prior contact with a law enforcement authority: federal, state, or local. Unfortunately, for whatever reason, these contacts weren't acted on in the proper manner. These contacts were the result of good old-fashioned police work, e.g., suspicious activities and/or behavior that alerted some cop to the terrorists. I know that those of us in local law enforcement did our job, but someone else at the state or federal level didn't do theirs. This lack of inaction should never be allowed to happen again.

You are probably asking yourself, "What does any of this have to do with building searches?" The answer to that question is this: It has everything to do with building searches because an active shooter, a bomb threat, or other types of violent or destructive incidents, AND a terrorist attack may require that you search a building or buildings, and you must be prepared for these and other possibilities.

Terrorism is REAL and we will be dealing with it for years to come. There are five basic things you must remember about a terrorist or terrorist cell:

1. They DO NOT NEGOTIATE.
2. They are PREPARED TO DIE FOR THEIR CAUSE.
3. They have no compunction about killing innocent women and children for their cause.
4. They will not hesitate to kill our law enforcement first responders and other public safety personnel.
5. They HATE THE UNITED STATES and Americans, and will do anything they can to destroy the United States and what it stands for.

The cold hard fact is that you and I are going to be the first responders to a terrorist incident, NOT Homeland

Security, the FBI, or any other federal agency that Congress has tasked to "fight" terrorism, so begin preparing yourself now, before it's too late.

A suspected terrorist activity should be treated with extreme caution. Most terrorists use explosive devices such as car bombs or satchel charges contained in boxes or other containers. These are now identified as IED's – Improvised Explosive Devices. Terrorists also arm themselves with extremely heavy firepower, generally automatic weapons. So much for the theory that claims gun control will stop criminal activity. Keep in mind that terrorists may use explosives and automatic weapons together to accomplish their mission. Don't rush into a situation and become a statistic! Your response should be extremely cautious, using the tactics you would use for a robbery in progress, an active shooter call, or barricaded suspect — with or without a hostage — based on your agency's policies. Try to consider all possibilities when you prepare to respond to your call. Terrorists have been known to set up ambushes for first responders outside the primary location of the attack, such as a bombing. They know that we will RUSH to the scene. They also know that our primary focus will be on taking care of victims, and by doing so, we will not pay attention to what is happening around the outer perimeter scene, thus presenting them with the opportunity to initiate a secondary attack either with explosives or firearms that will kill us and other first responders. Responding to calls of this type now requires us to establish a perimeter that allows us to look for and identify possible secondary attackers. In the past, our perimeter security was designed to ensure the safety of onlookers. Today, it is to also ensure our safety and that of other first responders.

I recall the lyrics of an old love song that said, "Fools rush in where angels fear to tread." Change those lyrics just a little and you can apply them to officer safety. "Don't be the fool who rushes in and becomes an angel." This may be a bit corny, but speed kills! Slow down. Officer safety is always first!

Keeping in line with my KISS theory, Keep it Safe and Simple, the key word in dealing with any call-for-service be it criminal, civil, public service, traffic accident, traffic citation, or possible terrorist activity, is SAFE! Add to my theory that AWARENESS equates to SAFETY! Be constantly aware or your environment. Pay attention to people, cars, and other things, when you arrive at the scene of a call, make a car stop, pedestrian check, or whatever. Look for the UNUSUAL and EXPECT the UNEXPECTED. I've told you to "Stop, Look and Listen," before making an entry into a building. These three words were never more important than now. If you're alone, slow down, stop if necessary to assess the situation, take your time and don't rush into an incident you are not prepared to immediately control. Look at the situation, what's happening? Listen to the situation: do you hear gunshots, yelling, screaming, etc. Don't be afraid to ask for help! Strength in numbers is a good thing, so long as those strengths are used properly. Most important, is the necessity of a good tactical plan and the buy-in and understanding of everyone involved in the operation: be sure everyone knows their role and area of responsibility. If you conduct a building search at the site of a suspected terrorist activity, be sure your search plan includes the possibility of booby traps and the presence of chemical or biological agents. If a specialized search team is not available, you need to include members of the bomb squad and hazardous materials units on your search team. Prior to making any entry, all known factors must be discussed, and any "suspected" factors must be identified and discussed. These discussions will enable you to answer the questions of how, who, and what will be done.

How, means how the search team will make entry and conduct movement through the building while looking for suspects, booby traps, and/or other physical hazards to the team.

Who, means what member of the search team will handle what aspect of a specific threat. For example, an EOD technician will handle bombs and booby traps and the team whose responsibility it is to conduct the search will handle suspects.

What, means what other members of the search team will be required to do while a particular threat is being handled by a specialist. If there is an IED, does the search team evacuate the building, the surrounding area, or what? If a suspect has been located what does the search team do with him or her?

Consider these scenarios. You get a call for a barricaded subject; is the subject an emotionally disturbed person or a terrorist? You spot a suspicious car or truck parked in front of a government building; is it a delivery or a car/truck bomb? You follow a car load of people, they're driving erratically; is the driver drunk, high on narcotics, or experiencing some type of medical problem? Could the car be full of terrorists who are trying to suck you into an ambush? You observe a person who is dressed strangely for the weather conditions or type of event approaching a large crowd of people. Is the person acting strange? Does he have a detached, blank look on his face? Is this person just a weirdo or a homicide bomber? What do you do?

Approach all incidents and individuals you encounter with an extra measure of caution. When you come in contact with someone who may be involved in some type of criminal or terrorist activity, you need to be sure you know with whom you're dealing, so run thorough checks. Also, make sure your traffic stops and pedestrian contacts are initiated with that same extra measure of caution.

We must remember that terrorists are extremely fanatical in their beliefs, and their organizations have demonstrated great resilience and adaptability in order to penetrate and defeat our security defenses. Since 9-11, terrorist organizations, and in particular our primary enemy Al Qaeda, have done many things to keep us off balance. Now, as in the past, their primary operatives have been males in their late 20's and early 30's. However, new intelligence indicates that Al Qaeda may be recruiting females to take a more active role in their attacks. They continue to recruit Middle Eastern extremists but have expanded their recruitment to include other Muslims who can pass as Europeans—presumably females as well as males. They are recruiting Muslim converts from other nations too, including northern Africans and southern Asians. Many of these "new" terrorists will be used to infiltrate the United States in order to locate, identify, and plan targets for future attacks. I share this information so you will avoid the trap of stereotyping what a terrorist might look like. They look like no one and everyone, so let your law enforcement training take over when you get that "funny feeling" that something isn't right, and act accordingly.

We all came together as a nation after 9-11 to fight terrorism. Today, however, even though others in our society are now wavering in this fight, we cannot. Our military continues to perform magnificently in our war against terrorism in foreign lands where the terrorists live and train to bring their terror to us. Never forget that you and I are the front line of defense against terrorist attacks on American soil. Each of you must apply all your skills in recognizing unusual behavior and unusual circumstances, and act on your instincts and training as professionals to stop acts of terrorism before they happen. We can't protect everyone, but being proactive in our endeavors to meet these new challenges is far better than being reactive to an incident where lives have been lost and terrorism has again shocked our nation.

It is no great revelation that terrorist training consists of a multitude of military style disciplines such as firearms training, bomb making, ambushes, building assaults, urban warfare, and assassination. Aside from these obvious areas of training, they also learn how to infuse themselves into their target's society to formulate and plan their acts of terror.

In general this phase of their training addresses the terrorist's mode of dress, lodging, how to fit into a neighborhood or business district, types of transportation to use, methods of surveillance and intelligence gathering, target selection and identification, counter-surveillance techniques, the clandestine use of cameras and recording equipment, managing multiple bank accounts, money laundering, etc., compiling intelligence into a reportable format, and how to avoid detection when bringing it back to their terrorist cell, organization, or country.

Remain alert, remain cautious, and be inquisitive about things and people. Seek answers, provide insight and information for planning, make decisions based on sound judgment and facts, and trust your instincts; if it doesn't feel right, it probably isn't. Finally, no matter what the situation or incident, your life and the life of your fellow officers is your top priority; your being killed is not an option! If you or your fellow officers are killed or injured while responding to help others, then all is lost! Remember what could happen to the fool who rushes in. Read everything you can to help you. Take all the classes and attend all the training you can throughout your career. Never stop learning and training. Sound tactics, good common sense, applied officer safety skills, and training are not signs of paranoia; they are the keys to your success.

It is my hope that this information will give you an edge in your war on terrorism, and keeps you vigilant when confronting persons you believe may be involved with terrorism, either actively or in support of other terrorist groups or cells.

INDEX OF PHOTOGRAPHS

INDEX OF ILLUSTRATIONS

About the Author

James Stalnaker is a Captain with a large Southern California Sheriff's Department with over 38 years of experience. He has been a deputy in corrections, patrol, and recruit training; a detective in patrol, homicide and internal affairs; a sergeant in patrol, and intelligence, as well as a team leader in SWAT; and the executive officer of the Training Division. He was the first commander of the Narcotics Multiple Enforcement/ SWAT Detail, and was instrumental in its inception of combining Narcotics and SWAT together. He is currently the Commander of a patrol station with two satellite patrol stations, and a Type I jail facility. He has been an active instructor since 1973 in officer safety, patrol procedures, building clearing methods, vehicle operations, investigations, court room testimony and other patrol and tactical related topics. Since 1987, he has been an active instructor in SWAT tactics, barricaded/hostage incidents, sniper tactics and psychological aspects of the law enforcement sniper. Jim and his wife Laurie reside in Highland, CA, and have two sons and a daughter and four grandsons, who are the light of their lives.

ORDER FORM

Toll Free: 800-732-3659
Telephone: 913-385-2034
Fax: 913-385-2039
Online: www.varropress.com
Postal: Varro Press, Inc.
P.O. Box 8413 • Shawnee Mission, Kansas USA 66208

Have your credit card information ready.

BUILDING SEARCH, *Tactics for the Patrol Officer*

Qty. _____ @ $30.00 each $ _____

Shipping: *
First book $5.00 $ _____
Additional copies $1.00 each $ _____

TOTAL $ _____

* Priority shipping or foreign: *Call 913-385-2034 or visit us online at varropress.com*

Ordered By:
Name: _____
Address: _____
City: _____ State _____ ZIP: _____
Country: _____
Telephone: _____

Ship To: *(If different from above.)*
Name: _____
Address: _____
City: _____ State _____ ZIP: _____
Country: _____
Telephone: _____

Payment:
☐ Check
☐ Credit Card
     ☐ VISA   ☐ MasterCard   ☐ AMEX   ☐ Discover
Card Number: _____ Exp. Date: _____
Name on Card: _____
Signature: _____